PRETENDING TO PRAY IN FRENCH

Elizabeth Podolinsky

Pretending To Pray In French

A Memoir

Cover design by Elizabeth Podolinsky

© 2016 by Elizabeth Podolinsky

All rights reserved

Podolinsky, Elizabeth

Pretending to Pray In French : A Memoir / Elizabeth Podolinsky. I Street Press : Sacramento, CA : 2016

ISBN: 978-1-941125-94-6

Library of Congress Control Number: 2017930005

PRETENDING TO PRAY IN FRENCH

Contents

INTRODUCTION 1

PART I 3

CHAPTER 1
ON THE FLOOR 5

CHAPTER 2
REMEMBERING PARIS 17

CHAPTER 3
FRANÇOIS 29

CHAPTER 4
FRANÇOIS AND ME 51

CHAPTER 5
ARRIVAL 61

CHAPTER 6
MOVING IN 65

CHAPTER 7
INITIATION 73

CHAPTER 8
LINENS 85
CHAPTER 9
THEOLOGY 91
PART II **99**
CHAPTER 10
STEPHAN / IRENE 101
CHAPTER 11
MONTPELLIER 115
CHAPTER 12
ON CONVENT TIME 127
CHAPTER 13
JEROME 133
CHAPTER 14
SISTER ROSE 140
CHAPTER 15
SECRETS 149
CHAPTER 16
SISTER JOSEPHINE'S CHOIR 155
CHAPTER 17
AGNES'S MUSIC 163

PART III **171**

CHAPTER 18
SHOPPING AT THE GAP 173

CHAPTER 19
HOLY THURSDAY 181

CHAPTER 20
GOOD FRIDAY 186

CHAPTER 21
EASTER 193

CHAPTER 22
EASTER MONDAY 203

CHAPTER 23
EYRES-MONCUBE 211

Acknowledgements 220
About the Author 221

INTRODUCTION

I dreamt that I was a nun, in full habit, walking like a proud queen through the courtyard of an ancient European cathedral, the long black skirts of my habit brushing lightly on the stones. Water dropped heavily into a pool in a fountain in the center of the courtyard. As I entered the cathedral through its open massive doors, I wondered why I thought about men anymore; I was a nun. It was a revelation to me, the nun, that I no longer had to think about how to get a man. It seemed a simple solution to all my anxiety: I wasn't allowed to have one. Calm strength hummed through my legs, up through my core and into the crown of my head, pulling me taller while rooting me into this ancient ground.

When I woke, the dream felt familiar, like an echo from the past, a left-over message. I felt like I should follow it.

PART I

CHAPTER 1

ON THE FLOOR

On the cold white tiled floor in the men's bathroom, I sat against the wall across from a line-up of white urinals, next to a bottle of bleach. The thick cotton fabric of my blue apron, the traditional style and color that French laborers wear, protected me from the pale urine stains that Sister Jeanne had assigned me to wipe off the walls.

A heavy plastic blue bucket propped open the bathroom door to prevent asphyxiation by the "Javel", or bleach. The liquid emitted a powerful eau de parfum to disguise its toxicity, a marvel of French chemistry. I imagined a subtitle printed across the bottle, under the word Javel: "Sublime by Jean Patou".

I angrily threw a wet grey rag across the brightly lit bathroom into the bucket. This was not what I had signed up for.

Back in January, when Sister Jeanne accepted my request to spend the month of April at the Couvent des Dominicaines des Tourelles, or Dominican Sisters of the Towers, in south central France, I imagined contemplating my life, constructing my future, and relocating my center, away from the distraction of sex - not scrubbing toilets.

True, her fax did explain that I'd work in the mornings in exchange for room and board as a "jeune fille au pair" whose description could include activities such as nannying, cooking, and cleaning. This "jeune fille" did not envision cleaning the men's toilets in the conference center of the Convent of the Towers, AKA, the Catholic work camp for single foreign women.

My fellow laborers were not happy either. Irene, little and round, and a university student from Norway, complained the most. "The nuns are cruel, and for no reason," she told me the day I arrived. She had been at the convent for two months and was ready to leave last month. I assumed that these young female European university students studying French would know the truth about this "semester abroad at the nunnery" but she seemed as surprised as I was about the drudgery we had to perform. She told me that the nuns accused her of being "coquettish" with a blonde pout and a petulant flip of her long tresses. Who was there to flirt with in this rural nunnery? she asked.

Agnes from Prague didn't complain. After we set up shop (buckets, rags and brooms) in a vacated guest room, she plugged into her Walkman and started scrubbing. Our team of three mopped the bathroom floor, sanitized the shower with a spray of floral bleach (with undernotes of musk), stripped the beds and left a set of clean thin white sheets on the mattress. Agnes's goal at the convent was to improve her French fluency to the level required by a French medical group. She wanted to land a nursing job in Africa with this team. She was in her eighth month and staying for several more. Her Czech accent was so strong that I couldn't tell how well she spoke French.

I assumed that the weekly lessons that Agnes and Irene received from one of the nuns expanded beyond what we needed to perform our morning maid duties. I too expected to improve my French fluency while I was here - but not in French cleaning vocabulary. Yet after just one week, I now responded to "find the mop (le balai)," "get some rags (des chiffons)," and "fill the bucket (le seau)." C'est dingue! I exclaimed, a pronouncement of absurdity and craziness I learned from Stephan, the only male "au pair" on our team.

A crisp female voice delivered an order in the hallway outside the bathroom door. A door slammed. These nuns weren't unfriendly but they didn't smile either. No time for small talk at this institution. They were an efficient bunch, especially the young ones, young being mid-thirties from the looks of Sisters Jeanne, Bernadette and Clare.

I felt a chill from the hard tile floor of the men's bathroom through the thin black spandex material covering my butt. The bathroom's white institutional lines, and now sterile state, contrasted with my funky yellow bathroom back in Santa Barbara, an added room to the garden level studio I rented in a large blue Victorian.

Three months ago, I stood in my small kitchen in Santa Barbara. The window's view contained an orange tree and the dark green hedge that separated my Victorian from the neighboring one. I crossed off to-dos from several lists I'd attached to my refrigerator door with magnets Eric had brought back from MOMA in New York, just before he left me. As I prepared for my three-month "sabbatical" in France, I imagined this convent in southern France as a medieval monastic retreat like the European cathedrals and basilicas of the 18th and 19th centuries that emit romantic puffs of mystery while nuns in full habit cross stone courtyards, like the one in my dream. But there was no "Sound of Music" aesthetic in this convent, circa 1970s.

Instead of the soulful surge I felt in Saint Sulpice Cathedral in Paris, an ancient monstrosity of beauty where I wandered between sets of pews on a cold afternoon just last week, the convent's modern geometric architecture left me flat and numb.

The architect's vision had produced five sand-white angular convent buildings hidden on a hill between bright limestone outcroppings and sycamores. The global Catholic building fund must have been flush in the 1970s, resulting in this modern convent. Its architecture reminded me of the church and rectory my Uncle the Priest had raised funds to build when I was a child. He then ministered from that perch to the student community at a state college in southwestern Minnesota.

A smooth-faced doughnut-shaped building housed me and my fellow "jeunes filles au pair", along with guests who paid to enjoy a spiritual retreat - no work assignment required. The largest building contained the small round chapel, also 1970s-modern, a large dining room with views of Saint Loup Peak, a huge commercial kitchen, small and large conference rooms, and a lounge with puffy old sofas, along with these men's urinals. Another building housed more paying guests and a part-time priest. The nuns' cloister sat in the center of the convent campus and was off limits.

And I was scrubbing the floors just like the nuns did in movies I watched on TV in the early 1970s as a young girl. But I wasn't a nun and I didn't want to be a nun, not since I was ten years old. I came to the convent for some time out, quiet and reflection; I did not sign up for the "nun for a month" package.

A bell rang to announce Laudes and the short mid-day Mass, the second of five religious services each day, none of which I attended, then lunch, which I did. For me, this bell was the twenty-minute warning until lunch was served. I rolled my heavy body off the bathroom floor, put the mop into the bucket with the rags inside, grabbed the perfumed bleach by its handle, and exited the men's bathroom. I could hear voices from the kitchen in the empty hallway, most likely the chef Jean-Pierre and his assistant Renée and one of the au pairs who Sister Jeanne assigned to help serve lunch to the guests. I pushed open the glass door with my butt and dragged the bucket and mop and bleach over the threshold. Outside, the bright Mediterranean sun beamed yellow warmth onto my face and my skin prickled in the heat. I inhaled a topnote of bleach as my nostrils sucked in the sage-scented air.

My feet crunched on the white gravel as I trudged toward the laundry room to deposit the rags. A black Mercedes and ruby-red Peugeot were parked against the building. They belonged to students taking icon-painting classes taught by a Ukrainian woman in the Artist Room that perched on top of the convent's dining room. One of the students was a blue-blooded matron with white coiffed hair and loads of pearls around her neck. She and her fellow students painted the Virgin Mary and Jesus on wood panels.

She wore a Chanel suit at lunch in the dining room and I imagined that her middle-aged skin was covered in creamy Chanel foundation. She and her friend smelled of subtle and beautiful perfumes that I couldn't breathe in enough of. These Hermès women spoke in proclamations about their friends in French that sounded hard and flat.

I dropped the soiled rags in the empty laundry room (the laundry nun was at Mass), then carried the bucket and mop to my building and shoved them into a narrow wooden closet. I hung my blue apron with dozens of other blue aprons, some tiny, some torn. Across the brown-tiled hall from the apron closet was my room, identical to the others in the building, anonymously lined up like soldiers behind white doors. The rooms bordered the outside edge of the doughnut-shaped building, with a hole in the center. Two toilet rooms and the closets with mops and aprons bordered the doughnut hole. The toilet rooms had a very small view into the hole containing nothing.

I opened the door to my room, number 27, my home for the month of April. Straight ahead, out the large square window in my room, a wild array of green pine and sycamore trees, a disorganized mess of dark needles and big flat leaves, felt like clean water on my face.

My mother would love this place, I thought sarcastically. This simple room was the modern version of the dorm rooms at the Catholic women's college my mother attended in the 1940s, and I later attended for a year in the late 1970s. But those rooms had a view of the Mississippi River bluffs in southern Minnesota.

The second and last lunch bell rang – no time for a shower or to change out of my black leggings and t-shirt, both covered in a veil of Javel and old urine. I washed my hands in the small white sink and threw on an oversized paisley shirt to cover my butt.

In Paris, where I had just spent cold February and March, I did care what I looked like. And instead of scrubbing floors and stripping beds, my rent included a cleaning lady who changed my bed sheets every Tuesday. The best were the heavy linen ones, soft from repeated washings. I imagined they had been handed down from Louis XIV, their luxurious weight holding me still as I fell asleep. Even the small holes in the fabric felt royal. The "femme de ménage" scrubbed the bathroom every week too.

I shared a two-bedroom 19th century Paris apartment building on Rue du Faubourg Saint-Honoré, one of the most exclusive neighborhoods in Paris. Every morning, my roommate went to work while I slept in. When I finally propelled myself out of the apartment in the late morning or early afternoon, I walked past the frozen mannequins in the haute couture boutique windows of Givenchy, Hermès and Lanvin, then south to the sixth arrondissement to peek into the windows of colorful shops and warm buttery bakeries. I drooled over the expensive linen dresses, crisp in yellows and pinks by Gerard Darel, calling to me from the windows that heralded the arrival of spring in Paris. But I didn't go into these shops; I had to ration the proceeds from my retirement fund that I had cashed in to live on during the three months I planned to live in France: two months in Paris, one month in the convent.

I loved Paris. I had studied French at the Institute Catholique as a college sophomore and had returned many times since. These three months were different: I wasn't going to be a tourist. I was actually going to live in Paris, find happiness, my purpose, maybe even a man. And when an acquaintance in Santa Barbara told me about living rent-free in the south of France for a month, in exchange for half a day's work, I booked the third month, the month of April, at this convent.

My Parisian roommate was sweet, beautiful and a countess. Louis XIV had knighted her family princes and princesses. However, my roommate's mother had married a count, which had taken the family down a royal peg. The family had no money but lots of property: a mill, a chateau, and this well-located apartment in Paris' 8th arrondissement. Despite her title, clear skin, long legs and ability to speak several languages, she suffered from being single at 34. At 41, I was her role model, a study in happy spinsterhood. She didn't want to be me, she just admired how "balanced" I was at my advanced age. And I seemed happy. Of course I was! I was in Paris!

When she interviewed me to be her roommate, she told me she would be out most nights at her tango class. Yet after I moved in, she rarely went out. One evening, we shared a healthy salad of endive and small lettuces, accompanied by seven different cheeses, she in her furry blue robe, ready for bed since arriving home from work at 7:00 P.M. We opened a bottle of red wine and she explained that she was going through "a passage". She wanted to marry and have children. Her twin sister had a husband and two children already. She had wanted to marry Pierre, an attorney. They had lived together for a while but that ended a year ago. She was very sad and waited for a husband to save her from this passage.

I was going through a passage too, despite my happy exterior. I still hurt from Eric's cruel break up with me a year earlier. I was angry too: we were going to get married, that's what I wanted.

Two winter months in Paris, and a brief romantic liaison, didn't heal my heart. It was up to the convent to do the job. The convent didn't feel like the wrong place to figure out life and love. But I couldn't see how cleaning rooms and urinals would give me any answers.

CHAPTER 2

REMEMBERING PARIS

The morning started like every morning the first week at the convent. I had breakfast duty so rolled out of bed at 7:00 A.M., met Irene in the empty dining room at the baguette-cutting table where several fresh chlorine-scented baguettes from the King David Boulangerie waited for us. They weren't very good, not like the crusty on the outside, chewy on the inside baguettes I consumed in Paris, at least once a day. Irene told me that there were two other boulangeries in town that made much better bread. I guessed that these baguettes from King David's were cheaper.

As the sun filled the room, Irene and I cut each baguette into inch-wide diagonal slices and stacked the discs in straw baskets. We placed several heaped baskets of bread, orange marmalade, berry jam and butter, on three long brown Formica tables. Sugar cubes waited in bowls for dropping into coffee. Granular sugar was only served at dinner at the convent.

Last night, like every night after dinner, we au pairs had set the breakfast tables before our workday was over. We placed an amber glass bowl for coffee, tea or chocolate, on top of a small amber glass plate which would hold the insubstantial breakfast of bread and butter and choice of jam or marmalade. Sharp knife on the right, small spoon to stir the morning beverage on the left. Everyone staying at the convent was assigned a napkin for the week and received a clean one on Monday. Last week's napkin was pink and small and wine-stained: I had spilled my wine at dinner. My new napkin was substantially larger – and stain-free.

After breakfast every morning, we "jeunes filles au pair" loaded the dishwasher with the morning bowls and plates, wiped the tables and set them for lunch. We then assembled in the sunny dining room to receive work orders from Sister Jeanne, our boss. This morning, Sister Jeanne assigned me to clean the urinals in the men's bathroom next to the conference room. Men visited the convent to participate in a retreat (next month's offering: Vers Sa Liberté Interieure: Le monde des passions – Freedom from passion?) or to attend Mass on Sunday with their families.

Sister Jeanne warned me that the urinals might take the entire morning. But if you finish early, she advised, you can check the large tables in the recreation room – they may need dusting. A group of young people from Montpellier would arrive tomorrow to do an afternoon course in catechism.

Meeting over. As we walked to the closets for buckets and aprons and I thought about how my lifestyle had changed since I arrived at the convent just over a week ago.

Almost every day and evening, for two months, I walked around Paris wrapped in a purple wool coat that protected me against the late winter wind. I walked miles in my heavy-soled burgundy Doc Martens lace-ups. Sometimes as late as midnight, I trudged up the five flights of black stairs, shiny from the concierge's immaculate care. My roommate was in bed already - she had to go work in the morning at a famous French perfumer that made use of her multilingual skills.

Under the grey skies of a February afternoon, I inhaled the beauty of a small garden and the small trickle of its fountain, hidden in the crazy mix of 15th and 20th century buildings, one stuck next to the other. I wandered through museums like they were forests. In the Musée de Carnavalet,

I thrilled to walk under high frothy ceilings painted with deep reds and gold and blues, flooding my senses with color.

In the evenings, I frequently attended a classical concert in a church. I scanned *Pariscope*, the thick little booklet listing the week's events, for a free choral or organ or chamber concert. One cold March evening, I walked to a church on Isle Saint-Louis to hear a boy choir. From the wooden pew, wrapped in my purple wool coat, I bathed in their Russian chant and the layered harmonies created by their pure treble voices.

I liked being alone. I didn't have to show up at work, share a cubicle, look at a computer screen, or answer the phone to again explain Santa Barbara's affordable housing program to a perspective applicant. In Paris, each day was open, with no plan until I made one that morning, or whenever I woke up.

I stayed up until midnight or later, drinking red wine or my roommate's Armagnac, then woke at 3:00 A.M. to a glass cascade of empty wine bottles being dumped in the trash at the Buddha Bar around the corner from our apartment.

I walked all day, distracted by the city's architectural grace, its sorrowful winter beauty, gazing at leafless sycamores as still as the dirt-stained saints who stood in stone at the entrance to the Church of Saint Sulpice. I watched beautiful men, tall, slim and confident, striding on wide boulevards near Place de la Concorde with open coats of fluid brown cashmere fabric. In the narrow streets near the University of the Sorbonne, they wore soft wool scarves wrapped around their necks, their dark eyes almost meeting mine.

I'd hoped to find him in Paris. I sat in a Jardin du Luxembourg café, empty and quiet under the overcast winter sky, wrapped in my purple wool coat, cradling a small green ceramic cup of warm Darjeeling tea. While the tea cooled, I hoped he would sit down at the little green table next to me. Little boys ran across the garden's open expanse, their high voices carrying like old letters sent a long time ago. I was ready; where was he?

But I wasn't ready. I didn't want to drown in love, not again. I wanted to be happy on my own for a while. Eric's rejection still stung. I had tried so hard to make him love me.

I made two friends while I was in Paris. Judy was the friend of a friend of my neighbor back in Santa Barbara. She was American, a translator, and had lived in Paris for more than 10 years. We met at different cafés near her apartment

in the Marais where she smoked Marlboros and told me about dating the men whose ads she answered in the hunting magazine personals. Georges was her current fixation. I thought she was too patient with him and gave him too many chances when he didn't show up or didn't call back when he said he would.

Louise was a friend of a different friend in Santa Barbara. She was young and single, desperate for a husband to give her a baby. We met at a rum bar on Boulevard Saint-Germain and she told me about a man she thought might work out. "He was really great, this guy, and a doctor too. We slept together and he said he'd call but I never heard from him again," she told me.

I could have used some more friends but I didn't want to hang out with American expats like the ones I met at Parler Parlor, a Franco-American conversation group I attended one afternoon. I wanted to meet French people, not pal around with my countrymen. I didn't want to be associated with that group. My translator friend Judy was an American, true, but not really. She didn't hang with the expats either.

But Judy and Louise were busy – they had jobs and lives. I had days and hours to fill. I structured my day around visiting an "important" church with notable architecture or medieval windows or famous dead inhabitants buried beneath its stone floors. One journey took me into the Rue Cler neighborhood where an afternoon market sold nougat, a chewy delicacy. I bought a large slab of the pistachio candy that looked like it was made in someone's kitchen.

Another day I took the Métro to the sixteenth arrondissement to see the Notre-Dame-de-Grâce-de-Passy church, founded in 1666. I found the neighborhood's exclusive shopping area and spent three hours in Franck et

Fils, a jewel-box women's department store. I walked to the third floor up an open staircase to Dresses. I ran my fingers along the fabric of the sleeveless linen dresses of pale yellow and blouses with bell shaped sleeves which grazed the wrist bone, all part of Cacharel's Spring 2000 collection. The saleswomen ignored me as I examined the finished seams on a crisp white jacket with a barely perceptible thin green stripe. I marveled at the perfection of the inside tailoring which was as stunning as the outside of the garment - for 1500 euros. I tried on hats, also stratospherically priced.

I drank an expensive cup of fragrant Earl Grey tea in the store's mauve-colored café where the tulips on each small table were different hues of purple. I was desperate to take something home with me from this dream emporium and settled on a pair of buttery leather gloves. Their functionality justified the expenditure.

On Saint Patrick's Day, I looked into the windows of a crowded Irish bar. It looked warm inside and people sat together drinking Guinness. I wanted to be with someone, anybody, to have a beer, to toast my mother's Irish side. I walked back to my apartment through the grey streets, and hoped I could convince my roommate to go out for a beer with me.

When I got home, my roommate was wearing a green facial masque and reading a magazine in her fluffy blue robe. I felt so tired all of a sudden. "I'm going to force you to go out with me and drink green beer, in your green masque!" I joked. She wasn't familiar with Saint Patrick's Day.

I called my father that night. "You have too much of your mother's Irish in you," he said. "Relax," he advised.

I wanted to go to a bar. I was desperate to connect with someone.

The next day, I trekked across the city in my Doc Martens to the Jardin du Luxembourg. I stopped to watch lotus flowers shimmer in a shiny pool of dark water in a rectangular fountain overseen by a stone cherub. It was so beautiful. I was so lonely.

I stopped at a patisserie next to the Louvre Museum and paid too many euros for a Napoleon, or mille-feuille. Seated on a wooden bench in front of the enormous Church of Saint-Germain-L'Auxerrois, I bit into its five layers of cream and raspberry, each separated by a crisp layer of pastry. The cream gushed out onto my hands and the pastry cracked, leaving broken panes upright and jagged in the cream. The cold afternoon wind carried traffic noise from the expressway that ran along the Seine and the diesel fumes mixed with the sweet berries on my tongue.

While I lived in Paris, I didn't keep up my twice-a-week mile lap swim and I didn't run trails like I did every weekend in the Santa Barbara foothills. I was consuming a lot of red wine and crusty baguettes and creamy cheese, with the occasional pastry. This new lifestyle made me anxious that I'd gain weight. I could hear my mother's disapproval of my overindulgence, even though she was thousands of miles away and I was no longer a teenager carrying an extra 30 pounds.

On one of the few occasions that my roommate didn't immediately don her blue robe as soon as she got home from work, we met at an art gallery to attend her cousin's art opening together. That morning, I had created an intention to get asked out on a date by Friday. Today was Ash Wednesday, a religious holiday I sometimes used as the start of a 40-day project.

Her cousin had produced a large book of lithographs with accompanying text. The cousin was a prince but looked like a former Ivy League college football player in his soft navy cashmere sweater, pulled over his very princely shape.

Gorgeous French men and women wandered around the modern gallery, holding glasses of red wine. I felt invisible in this forest of royal trees, like a wren that blends into the marshland. Even though my wool coat was Crown Royal purple, my short hair was light brown, flat and faded. I felt my face had already absorbed the makeup I had applied just before I left our apartment. Even though I spoke French well, I turned shy, like a country girl in the big city. How would I fulfill my intention to get asked out by Friday if I didn't assert myself?

My roommate introduced me to her cousin, the prince. He shook my hand and introduced me to his collaborator who had written the text to accompany the prince's lithographs. He was a professor, French, and taught at the University of Florida. He wasn't young or royal like my roommate and her cousin but a short middle-aged man with grey hair and big thick glasses. A grey suit hung on his slight frame.

The professor took my hand in both of his and said that he was enchanté - very happy to meet me. He held it in his warm hand for a long time and smiled at me. This physical connection felt visceral, like I was falling through the air. My language capacity left me - I could only smile at him. What did I have to say to him, to anyone? I felt foreign, a nobody.

I met another friend of a friend from back in Santa Barbara at the café in the Jardin du Luxembourg. He arrived in a short pea coat and jeans, tall and handsome with a Roman profile, like a descendant of the Hapsburgs, the aristocrats that my peasant ancestors lived under until they left for America in 1906. This 30-something American man told me he had sold his software company to a larger company and was staying for several months in his parent's apartment overlooking the Seine. We sat outside in our wool coats at the café painted a dark shiny color, not the green café on the other side of the garden. The air was balmy and soft for early March.

Crinkly lines burst out from his eyes, which I considered a good sign, and he liked to travel. He taught computer science, not a subject that impressed me. Like me, he was in Paris with lots of free time which he filled by planning and executing running races around the city with Australians and other Americans. The race required frequent beer stops along the course.

But an hour with him was enough. We talked about the difficulties of traveling with lovers, a fascinating topic, but the conversation wouldn't expand. Was his computer mind to blame? Or mine?

I drank more and more often. One night, I watched Whoopi Goldberg play a nun on TV, her voice dubbed into a soprano-pitched French. I sat on the floor of our living room, the TV on a chair, and finished a bottle of red wine. Irrational thoughts came to me: I love Americans! I miss them!

I felt ashamed that this was how I was spending my extended vacation and my limited savings: perusing the local wine shop for deals and drinking it alone at midnight. I scolded myself: I had so little time left in Paris - stop wasting it!

As the days evaporated, I thought about my options: remain single, working at some job, or marry someone who could add a layer of complexity to my life and occupy some of my time now consumed by anxiety about what to do with my life.

I made lists of things I wanted to buy before I left France:

Paint set (on rue Jacob)
Robe
2 bras (from Princesse Tam Tam)
Tea box (from Hédiard store)

Another list contained items I wanted in my life "soonish":

Apartment with high ceilings
Income of $100,000/year
Man that loves me, gets along with me
Jaeger clothes

I called the young woman who was subletting my apartment in Santa Barbara. Had I received any important mail, anything that might change my financial situation? Was my car was still in the driveway? Had a tree fallen on it?

Everything was fine, she assured me. Oh, Eric called, she said. I held my breath. Why did he have to intrude?

My left eye began twitching. My roommate told me to go read a book in the garden. "You do too much!" she cautioned.

I ducked into the Church of Notre-Dame-des-Champs on the Boulevard de Montparnasse to escape the noise and movement on the traffic-clogged street. This church had been named for a famous convent that provided refuge to Christians during the French Revolution. I lit a candle, one in the middle of the pack of white votives. I sat on a little wooden chair, surrounded by the heights of stained glass. Above me, the quiet space of the cathedral opened like a clearing in a forest.

I realized I was waiting to go to the convent. It was out there at the end of the tunnel, a result I assumed but resisted. But I still wanted Paris to work out.

On my way home from a choral concert which ended just before midnight, I crossed the Seine River from the Ile Saint-Louis. A moving wall of rollerbladers came toward me, filling the entire street. I ran around a corner to avoid being run over. They whizzed past me in the dark like a hoard of avenging angels in hot-pink feathered headpieces and silver short shorts.

I suddenly felt afraid. I was alone, vulnerable, easy prey. I didn't feel I could defend myself if I had to. I wanted to get out of Paris.

CHAPTER 3

FRANÇOIS

I had one more week in Paris before I would leave for the convent. On a cold Saturday in March, I ventured into the eleventh arrondissement, a neighborhood I didn't know, where Parisians lived and tourists rarely visited. The local library was hosting a poetry reading, accompanied by guitar. Printemps la Poesie: Springtime Poetry. I had found the notice in the national library's gift shop where I bought a little notebook covered with a colorful scene of Eleanor of Aquitaine on horseback.

I slipped into the library's large and crowded conference room, late. I sat on a table at the back of the room while the director of this library was introducing the poets, all men.

I scanned my program to identify the tall poet with curly grey hair and crinkly eyes. His dark eyes fixed on his audience and I hoped they'd fix on me. His body relaxed into the plastic chair on stage and his crossed leg exposed wing-tip shoes and cuffed wool pants - immaculately French. I wanted to sit on his lap. Jean-Louis had a substantial resumé and a Roman nose: long, narrow and distinctively French. Was he the sort of man that would be attracted to me? I wondered. Did his face have angles that complemented mine? The Parisian men I caught staring at me had round faces rather than angular ones, with small and round noses like mine. Most of this staring occurred when I passed Notre-Dame-de-l'Assomption, the Polish Catholic Church on my way to the Métro or to my neighborhood bakery to get a baguette on the way back to my apartment. Stocky men, young and old, milled around the courtyard in front of the church, hunched over with hands in the pockets of their jean jackets, like they were waiting to strike the factory.

Jean-Louis stood and began reciting a poem about the color blue. Looking down at the text, he made a mistake, shook his head, and asked himself aloud how that had happened, a little embarrassed smile on his lips. He was adorable.

When the poetry conference-concert ended two hours later, I slid off the long table. The crowded library conference room was hot.

Jean-Louis was surrounded by people, university types, at the front of the room. I wanted to approach him but felt intimidated both by his fans and his beauty. I couldn't think of anything to say to him so decided to locate a copy of the poems the poets had read.

"How can you wear that wool coat? It's so hot in here." I turned toward the male voice and answered that it was easier to wear it than to carry it. I moved my carrying arm in case I had used the wrong verb for carry.

He looked about 40, with thinning black hair, and round glasses on his round face. He was short, not tall like Jean-Louis, and wore a grey V-neck pullover over an orange collared shirt.

"Do you remember the last verse of the poem that mentioned something about an American?" I asked him. Everyone had laughed at this verse but I hadn't understood it.

The list of poems sat on a table. I remembered that the poet read it before reading "Crazy Horse", a poem I could follow.

"Can I remember?" he wondered, putting a finger on his small red lips. "Ah, as soon as I try to recall, the memory escapes me. Let me think…. perhaps something about American men preferring their locomotives to their women?" he smiled, but not at me.

Another French slam on Americans. What about those silly little deux-chevaux, the tiny cars that Parisians parked half on the sidewalk and half on the street, so small that you could probably move one out of the way with a good push? What did these cars say about the French male psyche? I wanted to ask him.

He picked up the list of poems. "Yes, here it is. 'Southern Pacific' by Paul Morand."

Les machines sont les seules femmes que les Américains savent rendre heureuses.

He looked up from the list of poems to greet a woman who was stacking chairs and carrying them into a room across the hallway. She was fair like me, plain, a little overweight, not like the French women in my neighborhood who sauntered on Ferragamo heels like fashion models.

I asked him if this was his library and he said no, he didn't own it but he did live in the neighborhood and so yes, this was his library. Now he knew I was not French. Or maybe my mistake was a common one made by the French too?

He picked up a stack of chairs and followed the woman. Was he involved with the plain librarian? He didn't have a ring on his finger.

The woman approached me carrying three chairs. I stood in my voluminous purple coat, like a deer in the headlights, blocking her path. She stopped, looked at me, and I moved back. As she passed me, I heard her breathing heavily.

Should I tell him that I had to leave? I didn't want to appear as though I was waiting for him to invite me to do something but I couldn't propel myself to exit. Maybe I should help with the chairs?

He walked into the conference room where he had left me and said something about breathing. Pardon? What? I asked. He wanted to get some air, the library was so hot. Yes, I agreed.

He picked up his jacket and I followed him out of the library into the overcast mid-afternoon sun.

I had to be bold or I might miss an opportunity! I scolded myself. I introduced myself. "My name is François," he replied. He extended his hand and smiled at me, his eyes magnified by his round glasses. His teeth were a little crooked and I wondered if modern dentistry had gotten a slower start in France than in the U.S. But Jean-Louis' teeth were straight and very beautiful. I guessed François didn't wear big steel braces like I did as a teenager.

We walked together slowly, in the direction of the Métro, I noted. I didn't want to get on the Métro. I'd spent almost two months in Paris and this was the first French man who wanted to talk to me, other than the Norman cheesemonger at my neighborhood farmers' market in front of the Église Sainte-Marie-Madeleine, a church that looked like a military tomb.

Every Monday, the farmer from Normandy taught me about the mysteries of his chèvre. He gave me samples aged to varying degrees. Sometimes I felt swindled when I thought I had said I didn't want that certain piece of cheese but he proceeded to wrap up two pieces for me anyway.

Swindled was a new word in my vocabulary. We had dissected it in yesterday's class at the Alliance Française. I

had signed up for the conversation class to give my days some structure and get me out of bed in the morning more than to improve my fluency. After class, drinking tea at the Three Colleges Café, I saw this word printed in *Le Monde* newspaper; something about a big scandal involving a French bank and an American insurance company. Sometimes I wondered if my roommate was swindling me with the egregiously high rent I paid her because I was an American and all Americans were assumed to be rich. I was living in one of the most expensive districts in Paris. I wasn't working. I had only five outfits to wear. That was not rich. I decided to be more open to being swindled as a cultural experiment and ended up buying lots of cheese. The cheese man strongly suggested I buy the expensive Pont L'Évêque for when I have people over for dinner. He didn't know that I'd later eat it by myself, standing at the counter in my miniscule kitchen at 2:00 A.M. I was happy that he thought I might actually invite people over for dinner.

One morning while I stood in front of his counter, he disappeared behind it, looking for something. I understood that I was to wait. I studied the huge face of Jesus printed on the banner that hung on the elegant but soulless Madeleine Church in front of me. Motor scooters whizzed around us and cars honked and the March sky was so hazy from pollution that a copper dome in the distance sat in a mist. The market was an island, physically separated from the hectic activity and noise.

The farmer reappeared and held up a 15x25 inch glossy color photo of his farm. The grass was green, the sky was blue, and red and brown chickens dotted the landscape. I pointed to the dead ones for sale in front of me, chicken meat next to rabbit parts. The barn was long and white, with little windows along the side. I had to clarify that all this cheese and these rabbits and chickens were from this farm, and that he made the cheese at the farm. Yes, he confirmed. I have some personnel though. Personnel. His teeth were long and brown. He told me that he and his wife leave their town in Normandy at two in the morning to get to the Madeleine Church market by 5:00 A.M. "2:00 A.M.?" I repeated. "Yes," he said. I wondered if I could get up early next Friday to be here when the market opened.

Please invite me to your Disney-perfect farm, I pleaded silently.

François's voice snapped me back to the library. "Would you like to have a coffee with me?" my new library friend François asked. An invitation! Of course! I yelled inside.

His invitation didn't feel icky like the Egyptian's who had tried to pick me up in the Tuileries Gardens recently. Mr. Egypt sat down next to me and told me that he was an architect, a Christian one too, who had recently lived with a woman who drank too much. He put his hand on my wrist, the only part of my body that was exposed. I was wrapped in my purple wool coat, Franck et Fils leather gloves on, arms crossed. This hand on my wrist gave him away. I saw the day-old beard, the white socks. He asked me to get a drink with him. "No," I said. "Are you afraid?" he asked. "No," I repeated. You're too forward, putting your hand on my wrist.

François was polite, seemed like a nice man, a regular Parisian. He was kind of cute, a little round, nice dark brown eyes.

"Which café?" he asked, while we walked and after I accepted gracefully and with composure. I felt overwhelmed by the idea that I would be sitting in one with someone, having a conversation rather than watching others have them. Though I did see Judy and Louise every couple weeks, I spent many hours drinking tea in Le Fumoir café, alone, reading *The Economist* magazine. Sometimes I feared I was losing my facility for human conversation.

I told François I didn't care which café. I pointed to the one in front of us and then to the one across the street. I was so giddy that I really didn't care though I was usually very particular about cafés. Choose a bad one and it stayed with me for a long time. I walked back and forth in front of a café, checking it out surreptitiously before I decided if it met my standards. I could tell a lot from the bathroom. I found that the quality of tea was positively correlated with the condition of the bathroom. Toilets with real toilet paper made me feel more confident about the quality of the tea I ordered. If I had to pull little squares from the dispenser one by one, I figured the tea selection wasn't going to be that good.

"The woman must choose the terrain," he said. "Terrain is more important to a woman than to a man so she chooses," he explained. I said something about women wanting to nest but couldn't find the word nest. Please just choose, I prayed.

He chose a café at the end of the street, one with golden beams overhead and beige walls. It was perfect, I decided, even before I checked out the bathroom. He asked me where I wanted to sit. Was this another terrain issue? I wanted to be more decisive but felt the hated pull of passivity. We stood together, just inside the door, me silent. "Let's sit there, near the window," he pointed. Apparently my terrain was outside and his was inside.

Beautiful Jean-Louis and his small entourage sat in the back of the café, Jean-Louis laughing, the center of his flower petals. But I wasn't interested in being a part of his adoring clique now. I had my own audience.

At our table for four, I took off my heavy wool coat and put it over the chair opposite the chair François had put his coat. He sat on the chair with his coat so that the arrangement had us sit diagonally across from each other. I held my breath. François moved his coat and then his body to sit across from me.

He ordered a hot chocolate and I ordered what I always ordered: black tea with milk. I was relieved that he didn't order a beer or glass of wine. That choice would have forced me to order the same, to match him. Though I kind of believed I spoke French better when I was slightly inebriated, I wanted to stay awake for this experience.

I had hoped I'd meet someone while I was in Paris; maybe this was it. But the timing was poor: I was leaving for the convent in a little more than a week.

I told him I was in Paris to write but since there was so much to do and see in Paris, I wasn't very productive. After many failed attempts to put my life's adventures down on paper (it seemed more important to check out the shoes at the Franck et Fils store), I was now attempting to write essays about churches I'd been visiting and the emotions their architecture evoked.

François wrote too. He had studied mathematics, once directed a company, and had lived in Africa. He now trained employees of a large multinational company. He said he had made lots of money as a director but then he changed his life and now made less money and did what he was told. He was much happier.

"You speak French very well," he said, three times. He then lectured me on methods to increase my productivity but redeemed himself by admitting that he used none of these methods himself.

"Did you know I was an American when we first spoke to each other?" I asked.

"No," he said. "When I first spoke to you, you seemed from Eastern Europe, not the United States. You don't move like an American."

I told him that my grandparents emigrated from Slovakia and my father spoke Slovak until he started school. François smiled with his new discovery.

I admitted that I didn't want French people to know I was an American. I was ashamed. I half-way retracted this confession. I wasn't really ashamed of being American, but embarrassed by Americans in Paris with their loud, flat voices. I was thrilled that he didn't lump me into that hoard.

"Do you think that the poem about American men preferring their cars to their women is true?" I asked.

"I don't know much about American men but...."

"What about French men?" I interrupted, surprising myself with my boldness but so happy that I could speak French well now.

He responded that when he was young, he hated the strictures of language because they prevented him from expressing what he wanted to say. I didn't interrupt him to repeat my question about French men and their autos. I also didn't contradict him by telling him that I loved languages and their rules. If I thought about it long enough, I might understand how the complexity of the French language might help me understand French culture. Maybe there was an answer in what François said about language that would clue me in on French men and their autos. Did I miss it?

During the three hours François and I sat in the café, he occasionally stared at the small paper receipt with the tea and hot chocolate prices printed on it. The first time he fixed his attention on it, I asked him a question to stall his departure. The second and third times, I stayed silent. Both times he started a new thought on his relationship with writing.

He told me his wife was dead. An old French song played over the café's speakers that I recognized. François said it was an Edith Piaf song from the 1940s. He said that his son liked this song but that he himself didn't like Piaf's music when he was young. Now that he was older, he understood it. His son? All of a sudden, François's life came into relief, like a face on a wall's surface.

I told him that I was leaving for a convent in a week and staying for the month of April. I hoped to do some serious writing there, free from worldly distractions.

He didn't comment on my announcement but told me that I was adorable. He stated it in a way that seemed ambiguous and since he said it in French, I couldn't assume his intention. Adorable could mean many things in French: there was a lot of latitude. The word was slippery and relied on context. What exactly did he mean? That I was cute? Cute but stupid?

It was dark outside when he paid the bill, after asking me if I would let him. Of course, I said, but immediately feared I had committed a French faux pas. Did I give him some signal that I didn't intend?

"Would you like to come to my house?" He said house, not apartment. I hadn't seen any houses in Paris. I was wary; the invitation seemed aggressive. Was he going to try to kiss me on the couch? Or did he invite me because I had nowhere else to go? Because my roommate had forgotten me?

I had plans to meet my roommate for dinner, this was true. But she wasn't picking up the phone at home. She hadn't called my cell phone either. I was worried. Should I go back to our apartment? Maybe there was a written message for me. Maybe the answering machine was broken. Maybe she didn't want to go to dinner and so was avoiding answering, avoiding me.

"Let me try calling my roommate again," I responded. I let the phone ring ten times. No answer. I was nervous – no one knew where I was. I could call Judy, my American friend. We had met for coffee only a couple of times - I barely knew her. And when would I call her? Secretly in the bathroom of the café? I felt I could take the risk: François was not a large man - I could probably defend myself.

François and I left the café and walked by doors that opened from the dark street into yellow-warm African stores selling food, colorful textiles or CDs. Glass and steel high-rise buildings loomed in the distance, so different from the graceful architectural lines of my neighborhood. All of a sudden, the village ended and we stood in a forest of apartment buildings.

François stopped in front of black steel gates that enclosed a modern high-rise apartment building and pushed numbers into a keypad which clicked open the gate. A young black man walked with us to the door of the apartment building and pushed a button next to an occupant's name. He asked François something and François responded that he lived on the second floor. The young man seemed unsure, suspicious. We got into the elevator and the young man exited on the second floor. The elevator door closed and we took the elevator to the third floor. There were no black men in my neighborhood.

François's door opened into a spacious, modern apartment with low ceilings that ended at a glass wall which looked out into a small rock-walled space filled with green ferns. I became conscious of my lungs and the possibility of moist air, absent in the sterile high-rise landscape we had just left outside. The apartment was filled with African masks and sculptures of black pointy-breasted women in twisted positions, some sitting on little tables, some large enough to sit on the carpeted floor. This confirmed my stereotype of French men: they like large breasts.

The apartment's rectangular sitting room with long low ceilings inspired calm, despite the breasts in every corner. Did he choose the terrain, or did his wife? I wondered how she had felt about all the breasts.

"Would you like a glass of juice or perhaps a whisky?" He took out a bottle of whiskey from a large wooden cabinet against the wall.

All of a sudden, I felt self-conscious about my reputation. It was the wrong choice to have a whiskey, offered by a man I hardly knew. "I don't really like whiskey," I said.

He told me that the bottle was six years old, offered only to guests. He didn't drink much. He was angry with alcohol because his wife had drunk a lot.

"Did she kill herself?" I asked, trying to keep the curiosity out of my voice.

"No," he replied. "Alcohol and smoking killed her." This seemed akin to suicide but I didn't say anything.

I remembered our conversation back at the café when he admitted that he was crazy about Emily Dickenson. He loved her poems; they expressed so much emotion, he had said. I told him that my favorite poet was Sylvia Plath, who had killed herself. He didn't know her work. I thought it was probably better that he didn't know that when I was 17, I revered a poet whose poems were all about anger and suicide.

He handed me a glass of orange juice and invited me to stay for dinner. Perhaps his son would be able to join us, he added.

As I sat down on the long black leather sofa, a young man came through the front door. He was tall, with a small beard under his chin. He looked French with messy black hair and delicate white skin. He smiled, walked toward me and extended his hand. I was impressed by his good manners, despite no mother around.

François told him there was a message from Emily on the answering machine. I wondered how François knew that; he'd been with me all afternoon. When did he check the answering machine? Maybe the son left early this morning, before François left for the library?

François and his son talked about going out for dinner but then I figured out they were talking about take-out options. I was offered a choice: pizza or Chinese. Chinese.

François said there was a good Chinese restaurant around the corner. I should come along so I could translate the menu. I imagined that his sense of humor could become annoying.

François and I walked for several blocks. The restaurant was not just around the corner so I may have misinterpreted what he said. I had rarely asked him to repeat anything he had said today but maybe I was getting tired from speaking and listening to French for several hours.

The streets were dark and quiet with no traffic. I wondered if there were any restaurants in this part of town, an odd occurrence in the city that invented them.

At the end of a dark street, I spied a beacon of light. The man and woman who ran the brightly lit Chinese restaurant shook François's hand and then mine. François introduced me. It seemed significant, this introduction. I felt I was auditioning for a role and wondered if he saw some future where I would someday run through these streets to retrieve a meal for François and me and his son.

I offered to pay for my dinner but François refused; I could pay tomorrow. I was startled. Tomorrow? Was this French flirting? Or did he believe I'd be here tomorrow? Maybe another failed attempt at humor?

It was quiet back at François's. His son had set the table. François looked surprised and I wondered if I were the rare female guest. François didn't seem like a major catch, though this was a very nice apartment.

I waited for François and his son to start eating or a cue that we might share our dishes. I didn't want to make them uncomfortable with my expectations. Did the French share Chinese food? I realized I was holding my breath. Maybe they were both as timid as I was. We didn't share.

My hot and sour soup was good but the chicken curry lacked curry. Someone once told me that Chinese food was much better in the U.S. than in France because the Chinese had been in the U.S. longer. I didn't understand that logic.

During dinner we talked about movies. His son knew them all, American ones too.

"Did you see any movies during Cinema Week?" I asked him. This French festival of film celebrated the art form by reducing the price of a ticket to about a quarter of the regular price for a whole week. I went to several films.

"No, I've been studying for my final exam; I take the test soon," he frowned.

"I saw 'The Talented Mr. Ripley' a couple of days ago. It was disturbing. I can't get it out of my head." I explained how the main character cons his way into a higher social class to assume his rival's identity. It ends in murder. I didn't tell them that I felt like the main character, the con man: trying to assume a new identity.

"That's with Matthew Damon, isn't it?" the son asked.

"Yes, you know him?"

"Of course! The French all know American actors," he laughed.

François said he'd never heard of Matthew Damon. He seemed old, all of a sudden, a doddering widower.

"I also saw 'An Ideal Husband' – I think it was British, based on an Oscar Wilde story," I added.

The son knew of Oscar Wilde, and so did François. I often walked past the apartment Wilde died in on rue des Beaux Arts. Wilde's Ideal Man - handsome, a loyal friend, and rich - resisted marriage. He, like me, had no responsibility to anyone. All I had to do was make sure my bank balance stayed above zero and maintain my hygiene. Other than that, I just entertained myself, like the Ideal Man did.

It seemed François hadn't seen a movie in 20 years but he did have something to say.

"In American movies, the man doesn't care about the woman and is always trying to get away from her. In French movies, the man is very attentive to the woman. Is this the condition between men and women in the U.S.?" François asked me.

This same subject had come up in my Alliance Française class on Friday. There were no men in the class.

I told François and his son about my class where we used our new vocabulary to discuss whether men are less attentive than they had been in the past. "When does the attentive period end?" our teacher asked us. Lubna from Russia said it lasted one month.

"What did you say?" asked François.

"It depends on the man, I guess," I answered. I wasn't going to reel off my list of lovers and where they had fallen on the scale of attentiveness. How long did Eric remain attentive? Maybe he never was, maybe I was just fun to have around. "My neighbor Monique believes that a man's attentive period lasts six months," I said. Monique grew up in Marseille and I wondered if geography made a difference. "She also told me that at the beginning of a relationship, she and the man she was dating would use the formal 'you' to address each other. Is this normal?"

Monique also admitted to me that she was sad when her date would start "tutoyering" her – using the more familiar address. In her experience, this shift happened soon after they started sleeping together and the mystery of romance had dissipated.

François's son laughed. "That's pretty old-fashioned - I don't know anyone that does that anymore!"

François didn't say anything. According to Monique, had François and I continued to address each other formally, that would have put us into a relationship category with potential.

At the café, I used the formal "you" when I spoke to François. He addressed me formally too. We kept it up until he called a "truce", right after we ordered our tea and hot chocolate. Could we tutoyer and use the familiar "you" with each other? he asked.

Before the revelatory conversation with Monique, I thought the formal "you" was only used to address the old, the famous, bakers, and train personnel that I bought tickets from, i.e., strangers. Since I mostly talked to people I didn't know, I always used the formal format.

I was on a roll - I had to know more about the complexity of French romantic behavior. And I had two subjects to do my research on, right in front of me.

"In Paris, I see a man, his face two inches away from the woman, speaking softly to her, touching some part of her coat, a button or the collar – are they for real? This attention, kissing in public, locked eyes – it's too much!"

I didn't know if I could handle such an intense level of attention from a man. I'd be afraid I'd be consumed by him.

François smiled at me.

I checked my cell phone to see if my roommate had called and saw it was almost midnight. I had spent more than six hours with François. In jolt of panic, I remembered that the Métro would stop running in about an hour.

"I should go home," I announced. All of a sudden I felt exhausted and struggled to find the French to complete my sentences.

François made me a cup of tea from black leaves in an orange tin. It smelled wonderful, sweet and dusty. He said it kept him up. I gulped down two cups.

François said he'd walk me to the Métro. He had to – I was lost in this neighborhood. His son smiled and shook my hand. "I hope to see you again." I felt flattered. His smile made me wonder if I had just been interviewed for a part in this family.

François and I walked down the middle of a dark street between two skinny sidewalks. A shortcut, he said. I couldn't conjure up anything to say. If he wanted to break the silence, he'd have to speak.

The entrance to the Métro was deserted. It was almost one in the morning. François turned toward me and handed me a yellow piece of paper with his name, address, and phone number on it. "I hope you'll call me," he said. François started to walk down the stairs with me. "If you're afraid, I'll accompany you to your destination," he offered. "No, I'm fine," I replied, and took a ticket out of my little purple backpack.

I didn't know whether to shake his hand or kiss him on each cheek. His brown eyes looked directly into mine.

"I'm free next weekend – or maybe we could get together during the week?"

I told him that I was going to my roommate's family's 17th century mill next weekend and that my sister was arriving from the U.S. on Monday and would be staying for a week. I was going to be busy.

I thought about telling him I'd see him in May, after I returned to Paris from the convent, but that seemed too cold. "Maybe next week will work," I replied.

He kissed both my cheeks and said he was "ravi" to meet me. Delighted to meet me! It sounded so much better in French than in English.

I fed the orange ticket through the machine and pushed my way through the metal doors and into the Métro's bowels. I didn't look back. When I rounded the corner out of François's sight, I laughed out loud to think that someone was "ravi" to meet me. Suddenly I was afraid that my happiness might show in this public place and that men would approach me. I opened my map of Paris and plotted the route to where I'd meet my sister on Monday.

CHAPTER 4

FRANÇOIS AND ME

I waited 24 hours to call him. I didn't want to seem overly interested but I wasn't going to be in Paris that much longer. Since I was leaving for the convent in a week, if François was going to work out, I had to find out now.

He answered, very politely. What happened to his enthusiasm at the Métro Saturday night? What happened to "ravi" to meet me?

But after that first conversation, he called every day, sometimes twice a day, and during the day too. I assumed he was at work but we talked for a long time.

He was fascinated with psychology and it dominated our phone conversations. I couldn't understand why he was teaching me, an American, about pop psychology. Of course I get it, François, I wanted to scream. I'm from America - we invented this stuff! I didn't know how to do sarcasm in French.

I was torn: though he treated me like his student, I liked having someone to talk to everyday. My membrane was thin. I had let him in, telling him how lonely I'd been in Paris. I confessed that I felt lost and hoped a month at the convent would help me figure out what to do with my life.

"I could love you, Elizabeth, because you aren't angry," François confessed to me on the phone, three days after our library meeting. Apparently François hadn't heard my admiration of Sylvia Plath and her angry poetry. He seemed to believe I was happy, pure, and childlike, a nice girl with normal desires and a healthy intellect.

My cell phone rang while I was wedged into a crowd of people vying to get to a bank of votive candles, all white in tall glass cylinders, flames moving like sheep grazing in a field. Merde. Cell phones were interdit – prohibited – in churches. I dug it out of my small purple backpack quickly; I was afraid of a cruel French reprimand. I was also excited; it rarely rang. Only five people in Paris had my cell phone number: my roommate, Judy, Louise and the friend of a friend who had lent me the phone while I was in Paris. And François.

"Hello?"

"Hello, Elizabeth", François cooed into my ear.

"Wait - I'm in a church – let me walk outside," I said.

"Elizabeth, my dear. I have to tell you - I wrote a beautiful story last night." When we sat at the café after the poetry reading, he told me he wrote technical computer manuals but wanted to write more creatively. "I want to read it to you when we're together." Was I his muse? I wasn't going to be anybody's muse.

While he spoke, I imagined him cradling his phone as though he held my hand, caressing it. Is this what a French man said to the woman while fondling her earlobe in the café?

Sometimes I didn't understand the French he spoke. When I asked him to explain what he meant, he was overly patient, as though I were a child. "Ah, Elizabeth, you are so sweet, not understanding. Let me help you."

I began to suspect that that he used the language to confuse me. Was this his idea of a French lesson? I considered myself pretty fluent after living for almost two months in Paris.

His manner of speaking began to annoy me. I could see his little red lips pursed like a schoolteacher's. A little man with a penchant to instruct.

I started to wonder if I might be crazy. "François, I feel like you're playing with me," I said to him on the phone.

I wondered if he hated women.

Then my sister arrived from Minneapolis. Like me, she was also a Francophile, had studied in Paris like I had but she had two young children. She had just been offered a job and the promise of future income convinced her to visit for four days. I was so happy to see her, to speak English, and to be with someone who had known me for more than two months. I didn't talk to François as much while she was here – we were too busy with Paris and each other.

He left messages on the answering machine in my apartment. My roommate told me that she didn't like his voice.

When I told my sister about François, she gave me the response I'd heard from her many times: "Liz, there are lots of fish in the sea; let this little one go." What did she know?

She had divorced, was busy with two kids, so no time for dating. She didn't know that there weren't that many fish, in the water or out of it. She wasn't in the fishing industry – I was.

The night before my sister flew back to Minneapolis, François said he wanted to see me. I hadn't seen him since meeting him at the library a week ago. It didn't seem odd that our relationship had taken place on the phone. It was an intellectual exercise, good for my French language skills. Maybe that's what this was all about.

François wanted to meet me for hot chocolate at a café in my neighborhood. Monique from Marseille told me that we'd find a good café on the Rue de Rivoli side of the Tuileries Gardens. The Seine River side was not as good, she said.

I didn't want to meet François but felt I owed him something. He wasn't it. I wanted a happy man, one who laughed, with crinkly eyes. I wanted an attractive man, like Eric. Why did he bug me so much? Why did I attract such weird men?

I told François to meet me at the entrance to my building's courtyard at 6 P.M. that evening. I didn't want him to come upstairs to my apartment. I stood under an eave, out of the drizzling rain. He came around the corner, not seeing me, holding a bouquet of lavender roses.

"François!" I called out.

He stood before me, pigeon-toed, a few inches shorter than I remembered, wearing the same grey pullover he had at the library. He stood in scuffed shoes, his bouquet of lavender roses between us. His hair was wet and his shiny eyes reflected me, like the prize he'd won at a science fair. I froze: how to respond to this man who was ready?

I didn't know if I should greet him the French way with an air kiss on each cheek, or like an American, a quick A-frame hug, only shoulders touching. I quickly took the roses. "Wait for me, I'll put these in water and be right back down. I'd invite you up but my roommate's not feeling well."

The roommate's adverse mental health had taken up lots of conversation between François and me over the past week so this was an easy excuse. I ran up the five flights of stairs and rang the doorbell. I didn't have the strength to insert the key and push open the heavy shiny black door. My sister answered. "Could you put these in water? It's too much," I rolled my eyes.

I ran down the five flights, around and around. He was waiting for me, smiling like a happy boy.

It was now drizzling heavily. I had an umbrella but he didn't so I didn't open mine. I didn't want to negotiate the process of sharing. I didn't want to get close to him. I kept my arms crossed in front as we walked toward the Tuileries Garden. Don't try to grab my hand, I thought.

We walked several blocks in the warm wet rain, both wearing glasses that got spotted with water.

We ordered hot chocolate and drank it silently in the empty café. I sat on my hands and watched the rain hitting the glass windows, making the spring greenery of late March drip like watercolor.

I avoided meeting his eyes. When I did look at him across the table from me, his eyes beamed into me. He leaned forward, like a happy but restrained puppy that knew I held a treat for him. I wanted to flee.

He offered the dream: living in Paris, being adored, someone smart. I liked his son. I could have jumped in, said yes, I'll stay.

I remembered the last time I was given a similar offer, when I could have jumped in, said yes, I'll stay.

Four years earlier, I had ended a year-long engagement to Paul. The engagement ring, his grandmother's, platinum silver encrusted with diamonds, was sparkly and gorgeous on my finger.

I took him to Minnesota to meet my family. In a lake cabin near Ely, he made pancakes for my recently-separated sister's delighted children. She looked at me incredulously: I had found gold.

Paul was ambitious; he finally had a good job and now he wanted the good life: wife, house, family. We were both 36, just the right age to marry. I would melt into his plan, like butter sitting out on the table on a hot day. My activities and thoughts would flow to his interests and ideas. I could fall asleep, confident he'd take care of me.

Several months into the engagement, my worried friends bribed me to make an appointment at Rumors Bridal Shop to try on poufy white wedding gowns by promising margaritas at Las Casas Bistro after.

But I couldn't see that future with Paul. So I stayed awake during our engagement, clinging to my own interests and ideas.

After the margaritas and wedding dresses, he and I spent a weekend looking for an apartment to share. We drove up into the Riviera of Santa Barbara that overlooks the ocean and walked through hovels in which Paul could barely stand up, tiny living spaces smelling of mold, for so much money. It was hard to find a place for two, not just for one, not just for me.

He started to smell sour. His clothes were always stained. His breath was rank, he smoked.

I contacted a former therapist and asked her to help me decide what to do. How can I know? I asked, terrified because both decisions – to marry him or end the engagement - felt wrong.

At the end of a concert at the Lobero Theatre, Paul and I cautiously walked between two rows of red velvet seats toward the middle aisle, avoiding the broken ones that blocked our way out. My heart beat fast and my body buzzed with electric energy as though I was plugged into a wall socket. What I wanted to say was stuck inside. But then he started, "When we're married...." Unformed and unrehearsed, I blurted out, "I don't want to marry you!"

Several weeks after I gave the engagement ring back, I bought a fake diamond one at Nordstrom's, a very good replica. I only wore it at home, when I was alone. The glass pieces fell out one by one and I eventually got rid of it.

I missed that diamond engagement ring, a public declaration that I was loved by someone, a gushy-warm feeling. I was part of something more than just my needs and obsessions. But the ring came with a commitment I couldn't make.

François wasn't asking for a commitment but I felt the same: trapped.

I looked at François, at his pilled sweater, his oily hair. A different kind of messy.

"I have to go," I told him. "My sister's waiting for me. She leaves tomorrow."

He called the next day. "Elizabeth, let's go see a movie," he suggested. He liked me. Of course he did. I was nice, I listened. I felt sick to my stomach.

I had told him a lot about myself, maybe too much. I couldn't imagine sitting next to him at a movie. I saw his next move: putting his hand on the collar of my purple coat, telling me how adorable I was, and how he could make me happy. Just like those couples whose faces allow only half an inch between them, breathing each other's breath.

"I'm busy François, I have so much to do before I leave for the convent." I knew he could hear the lie in my voice. I could have squeezed a movie in.

"Goodbye, Elizabeth." Clipped, punched in a soft way. He didn't even argue. I felt scolded. He took a risk, it didn't work out. Life goes on.

I stayed awake that night, staring at the lavender roses next to my bed. They were perfect in color and shape but had no scent. They were beautiful but a symbol of disconnection, not love, like my fiancé's ring. Though it was stunning, it was hard to tell the real one from the one from Nordstrom's.

On the last day in March, I said goodbye to Judy and Louise, the two friends I had made in the two months I spent wandering Paris. Judy was happy to store my Crowne Royal purple wool coat for me while I was away in the sunny south – I wouldn't need it there. Louise declared that I'd had the complete French experience by meeting a man, even though it didn't work out.

My roommate and I drank two bottles of Anjou wine with dinner, a huge salad of endive and delicate lettuces from the Madeleine Church farmers market, and the exquisitely delicate and soft Pont L'Évèque that the farmer said I should share with friends. My roommate wore her blue robe and I wore a green Chinese silk robe that I'd purchased at Franck et Fils, my favorite clothing store. My sister had bought one too.

The next morning, hung over, I got on a train to Montpellier, 500 miles south of Paris, toward the Mediterranean, to the convent.

CHAPTER 5

ARRIVAL

The train pulled into the Montpellier train station, into air that was warm and soft. I searched the crowded passenger arrival area for a nun's black habit and then walked the blindingly sunny parking lot. But Sister Jeanne wore a blue denim dress and smiled. She was young, maybe 35. Pear-shaped and plain. Her hair was cut short, coarsely shaved up the neck, light brown like mine with little gray strands sprouting from the top. She shook my hand, her round face smiling, and apologized for being late.

I wedged my bags into the back seat of an old, small white Peugeot that smelled of dust and age. Stacks of white plastic chairs that Sister Jeanne had just purchased for the convent's garden secured my body. I was wrapped in thick dark leggings and a heavy brown tunic. The sun's heat made the car feel like an incubator.

Sister Jeanne introduced me to Sister Christina, who sat in front. Sister Christina had just arrived on a train from Stockholm. Sister Christina had short hair too, faded jeans stretched over her heavy stomach and thighs, pale blue eyes, and a double chin. I wondered if she joined the convent because she had no marriage options. Just like me. Would I look like a nun, like Sister Christina, after a month at the convent?

I strained to hear their French dialogue over the car's buzzy European motor. Sister Jeanne explained to Sister Christina that she took her first vows in 1991 and had been a nun for 11 years. The math didn't work.

I didn't care that I didn't understand what they said. Though my body was scrunched into the back seat, pinned between the plastic chairs, my spirit stretched out in the warm southern sun. I felt my bones drop into gravity. My shoulders released their load.

We passed French trees with large green leaves and gray dappled trunks. The car stopped and started abruptly, winding through the cement barriers of a construction project and midday traffic. Dark-haired people walked slowly on the sidewalk on the other side of the barrier, smiling, wearing light jackets. Some sat low in small café chairs, smoking with no urgency.

Through the small backseat window, the warm Mediterranean sun and soft wind bathed me, washing away the train-lag of five hours of cigarette stench and cell phones and gray, hard Paris. I sat back in the wind, like a happy Labrador.

I had finally arrived.

CHAPTER 6

MOVING IN

As the little Peugeot strained to reach the top of a steep hill, a large white building, starkly modern and geometric, circa 1970, came into view. The car slowly crunched over white gravel and stopped in front of a row of cypress trees. Tall leafy sycamores with bleached and mottled trunks saluted lazily like a welcoming party. Next to a large boulder, I spied two plastic white chairs, just like the ones that trapped my body in the back seat incubator.

I pulled my body and my two suitcases out of the backseat and followed Sister Jeanne who carried a white plastic chair in each hand. We walked toward a two-story vanilla colored round building. Where was the medieval aesthetic I saw in my dream?

She opened a glass door to the vanilla building and signaled me to enter. The dark hall was empty. Where was everybody?

"Voilà, votre chambre." Sister Jeanne introduced me to my room as she opened the slim white door with a skeleton key that waited in the lock. Its turn echoed sharply in the dark and empty hallway. Was I the only guest staying in the doughnut-shaped building? Were there others behind any of the other identical white doors?

The room was small and spare. This layman's cell had a sink, a shower, and a narrow bed in the corner against a white wall. A small, simple wooden desk sat under a large square screenless window which brightened the white room. My stomach tightened. How was I going to contemplate my future in such a simple, uninspiring aesthetic?

From the window, I saw a field of thick black stumps, low to the ground, and wondered if they had died. Like a movie backdrop, a forest of sycamores and pine trees blocked any view.

"Voilà, je vous laisse, I'll leave you now," Sister Jeanne said. She turned, leaving me efficiently, like a warden in her shapeless blue denim frock.

I gently pulled the weightless door shut even though the silent building felt deserted. The room smelled as sterile as its pure white walls, as though rinsed with bleach-diluted water. No rug covered the hard ceramic brown tiles. I was in Languedoc, a region storied with medieval knights roaming the limestone hills and hermits holed up in caves. I believed that Europe offered a spiritual balm for my secular wounds. I came to absorb the musty interiors of cathedrals, to stand on ancient land where religious history was made. The ground felt holy over here: Blood was spilled for God.

I wanted my infirmary more cozy, more earthy. I wanted the convent from my dream. I felt stripped of the typical Catholic medications: no holy water here, no bloody Jesus hanging on the cross over my bed. There weren't even curtains to soften the space.

I opened the narrow desk drawer. Several paper brochures covered the bottom. "Bienvenue," or Welcome, announced itself in black type on a thin orange tri-fold piece of paper. Welcome to The Dominican Convent of Sainte Marie des Tourelles – Saint Mary of the Towers.

I scanned the brochure. I began with the text "Reprendre Souffle": To Catch One's Breath. This convent community promised to deliver the time and space to reflect on my values. The community wanted to make my life more human while I was here by offering welcome, peace and silence, while recognizing that life was sometimes difficult and agitated. I sat on the edge of my little bed and wondered why I felt anxious. This was exactly what I wanted: I had come here to seek respite from the anxious activity of a 21st century single woman. I wanted to be a child of God, not a woman drowning in her desire for a man. I wanted to give that a rest while I was here in this place.

I picked up another brochure labeled "Bonjour et Bienvenue chez les soeurs Dominicaines des Tourelles" AKA "The Rules." "The Rules" were printed on a pink sheet of paper and they were for me, one of the foreign guest workers at the convent, or "jeunes filles au pair."

"The Rules" stated that the nuns will try not to abuse us "jeunes filles" with overwork. The nuns are here to provide us with religious guidance, if we need it, and one-on-one

French lessons, if we request them. And they promise to throw us a party every two weeks - this appreciation because we help the nuns with the room and board services the convent offers to guests who come to the convent on retreat. In exchange for our labor, we get a room and three meals a day. We can also take advantage of the religious seminars that are held here, and listen to the guest speakers that pass through. They hope to create a family atmosphere for us but no mini-skirts or shorts allowed. The treatise ended with "to be a 'jeune fille au pair' at the convent is a true adventure!"

I didn't want a family or an adventure - I wanted to be left alone with my thoughts, to plot the rest of my life from this quiet perch in Languedoc.

"The Rules" also warned that after 10 P.M. at night, one must be absolutely quiet: no flushing of toilets after 10 or before seven in the morning. This rule made me nervous. What if I throw up at midnight or have diarrhea from eating too much Brie and Roquefort and drinking too much wine – was there an exception?

I slid "The Rules" back into the small wooden desk drawer but left the "Reprendre Souffle" brochure on top of the desk.

I looked out at the thick green pines and leafy sycamores that stood still in the dry warm air. Cicadas chirped loudly in the bright afternoon sun. I looked down at the orange brochure again and took a deep breath of the lavender, sage and dry pine that wafted through the open window. It smelled like Santa Barbara, my home.

Only two months ago, I stared at the Los Angeles-Paris roundtrip ticket stuck to the door of my refrigerator with a magnet that Eric had bought me at an exhibit at the Museum of Modern Art in New York City. It was late, so quiet upstairs - no more yelling from the drama-queen single mother at her three young children who lived above me. My cat blinked slowly at me from the sofa and turned away. I sat down next to her and pulled on her dark caramel fur. She didn't know that she'd be living in Redlands with a friend for the three months I'd be gone.

I walked over to the kitchen table, covered with papers. My to-do list was as crossed-off as it was going to get: I had quit my job, sublet my apartment, and cashed in my County retirement fund. My flight from Los Angeles to Paris would leave in two days

It was too quiet - I had to move. I grabbed my keys and headed out in the dark on foot, up the long driveway to the street. I climbed wide and quiet Grand Avenue, jogged down the middle of empty Orena Street, past the dark Santa Barbara Mission Rose Garden, ran in the middle of Junipero Street between houses as big as ocean liners and slowed on Los Olivos Street as I approached the Monastery of Poor Clares. One light shone through a window on the second floor of the small convent, illuminating what looked like an empty hallway.

Santa Barbara's Poor Clare nuns walked barefoot, buried under layers of brown and gray fabric that exposed only white feet and faces. They weren't allowed to talk, only sing. At the daily 7 A.M. Mass, they hid behind a scrim and chanted in high wavering bird voices that sounded little used. Like castrati, their voice development had been arrested when they entered the convent.

I didn't go to Mass at this convent; the priest had a pre-Vatican II mentality and lectured the elderly parishioners about the evils of abortion and other sins committed by women. Instead, I sat in the monastery's empty little chapel on too-bright afternoons to hide from the sun's constant spotlight in always-sunny Santa Barbara. I sat in a wooden pew like a precious gem contained in the silent jewel-box chapel. Creamy yellow walls separated the line-up of thick stained glass windows donated by the rich and Catholic of Santa Barbara.

From the dark street, silent and fragrant with rosemary and jasmine from the monastery's manicured garden, I imagined a dormitory and wondered if the nuns shared a bathroom of shower stalls and cold toilets down the hall from their cells. I longed for that deprivation; it seemed romantic. I stood on the sidewalk, in the quiet and dark neighborhood, and yearned for the simplicity I imagined they lived in.

From the sidewalk in front of the convent, I watched the remaining light in the building go out.

CHAPTER 7

INITIATION

"On commence avec des noms des soeurs," Sister Jeanne announced. We'll begin your initiation by listing the names of the nuns living at this convent of The Towers. Maryam and I sat on straight-backed wooden chairs at the table on Sister Jeanne's left, up in the Artist's Room.

The Artist's Room had windows on three sides. Old turpentine hung in the square room, its toxicity damp and soft like a piece of linen whose stiffness yields with repeated washings. Sister Jeanne smoothed several pieces of paper with her hand against the table we sat at. Its rough surface was stained with blue, yellow and red splashes of paint.

I could almost hear conversations through the floor from the dining room below but the view was much more interesting. Pic Saint Loup - Saint Loup Peak - dominated the view to the west, a giant wedge of stained limestone that leaned like a cresting wave. To the south, an old red brick silo sat in a yellow field of mustard.

Maryam and I were the newest "jeunes filles au pair" arrivals at the convent. Maryam lived in Germany, a product of Turkish Muslims, small and dark with heavy dark hair whose beauty was overwhelming when she was still but made no sense when she walked, pigeon-toed and bouncy, her head upturned and a big white smile on her young face.

Maryam had no experience with Christianity. She had come to the convent to immerse herself in the French language, like the other foreign young women I worked with. She planned to stay for six months, twice as long as the minimal stay required by the convent, to receive weekly French lessons from one of the nuns in exchange for housekeeping work. Unlike the other "jeunes filles au pair," I was only staying a month and I did not sign up for French lessons. I was also 20 years older than these university girls who were majoring in French back in their home countries.

Maryam was ready to leave only two days into her "contract". She whined and complained. She had a boyfriend back in Germany and she missed him. "The Rules" allowed him to visit her but only after two months, the length of time recommended by the nuns for optimal acclimation to the convent and after most of the ache of homesickness had subsided.

Sister Jeanne began our initiation by writing Sister Genevieve's name in curvy French handwriting at the top left of a dark yellow piece of paper. The other side of the sheet was printed with an invitation to the convent for a day of reflection and prayer to study "a love the most grand" from First Corinthians 13. Bring your own lunch and Bible.

Sister Jeanne looked so young, like a girl. What was she doing here? I didn't know that young women joined the convent anymore. In Santa Barbara, I'd only seen old women wearing habits at the Old Mission or walking near the parochial schools.

"Sister Thomasina, 'accueil le matin', welcomes guests to the retreat center in the mornings," she explained. Her job included sitting in the central building's small office, taking payment for lodging from the guests, and selling them a small bottle of water or a Coke or a card with a photo of Saint Loup Peak pasted on it.

"Sister Catherine, 'accueil l'apres-midi', performs this ritual in the afternoon," Sister Jeanne explained.

"Sister Marie-Louise is blind and does the ironing, 'repassage'," she continued, penning Sister Marie-Louise's name so fluidly that I wanted to take a nap.

I wasn't sure how blind Sister Marie-Louise really was. The day after I arrived at the convent, I entered the room containing the ironing board and left Sister Marie-Louise a note on a scrap of paper on the ironing board asking for her permission to use it. Sister Clare, a sighted nun and her co-manager, personally delivered the news: "Sister Marie-Louise has granted you permission to use the iron and its board, as long as she isn't ironing." "In addition," she warned, "You must turn off and then unplug the iron and leave it in the exact place you found it." As directed, I put the iron back in its little metal cage attached to the side of the ironing table. I feared that any deviation would be calamitous for the blind nun.

Sister Clare co-managed the linens, "le linge", with Sister Marie-Louise. Sister Clare did not cut her hair short like the other nuns and it hung long and thin and brown down her back with broken gray hairs sprouting out around her pudgy face.

I sat across from Sister Clare's mother at dinner. Mother visited her daughter often. I had assumed that nuns gave up their families upon entering the convent, replacing the family with Jesus and their nun sisters.

Sister Clare walked with her large round belly forward, bouncing from side to side. Her bratty loud voice hurled cruel comments, scolding and issuing warnings. I avoided her.

I had expected the nuns to be evolved. They spent most of the day praying – why were some of them such bitches? They lived in the peaceful countryside, near the Mediterranean, where the sun was warm and lavender and sage and orange poppies grew up next to the convent buildings. I didn't get it. This convent could have been mistaken for a dormitory of hormonally-hyped female college students.

The nuns invited us "jeunes filles au pair" to eat lunch with them in their sunny dining room on Sundays at the convent. We didn't clean rooms on Sundays – we only cleaned dishes and served platters of food to the guests and ourselves, running from the kitchen to the dining room and back to lunch with the nuns.

We sat on white wooden folding chairs around six white tables and ate paella that Jean-Pierre the Chef prepared for this special Sunday lunch – Palm Sunday. This surprised me since it was still Lent, the 40-day period of suffering as Jesus did before being nailed to the cross. We still had another week until Easter. The food the chef served was usually simple, to remind us of Christ's suffering during this season. But this paella was glorious – filled with small shrimp, chicken and spicy sausage, causing a rare and almost obscene taste sensation. Saffron subtly flavored the yellow-stained rice and the whole yummy mess filled a large blue and yellow ceramic platter.

As four of us "jeunes filles" entered the nuns' sunny dining room with a view of a large garden outside the floor to ceiling window, an old nun stood up and welcomed us: "Bienvenue - here come the young ones!" Sister Clare snorted and looked at me.

True, I was not young. I was not old either; I had just turned 41. But I felt too old to be here, at a convent, on my hands and knees scrubbing floors (though more often with a mop), dusting side tables in the lounge, and loading dirty dishes into the commercial dishwasher after every meal. I should be married. I should have a big job with big money. Instead, I rolled out of my low narrow bed every morning, put on a pair of stretched-out black leggings, buttoned an oversized shirt that hung long to hide my butt, and squinted in the bright morning sun toward the dining room to prepare breakfast for the retreat guests with the other "au pairs". I felt embarrassed.

"Sister Patrice is responsible for the liturgy, 'liturgie'," Sister Jeanne continued. This confused me; I thought only priests were allowed to perform this scholarly job since it had to do with performing the Mass, a ritual reserved for men.

Sister Patrice was responsible for Marguerite, a postulant, a sort of nun-in-training, with laundry duties: "Postulante et buanderie". I'd heard that Marguerite had several grown children and had divorced her alcoholic husband. Whenever I saw Marguerite, she was working like an intern who wants a paid job. She didn't smile or speak. Her pockmarked face and convent haircut - a short chopped style - presented suffering, maybe by an abusive husband. This Dominican community would soon decide if she could become one of them and stay forever.

Marguerite worked in the laundry room. I saw her when I dropped off bed linens that a guest on retreat had stripped from the bed and folded so neatly that they looked like they hadn't been slept in at all. She was always bent over, in a white blouse and navy skirt, intent on something in one of the large grey sinks.

I looked at Marguerite's pitted complexion. Though I'd been told that I had good skin, I didn't believe it. I still saw the scars from my adolescent acne that tetracycline didn't erase and left my teeth slightly grey. Maybe they meant that my skin looked young, unlined, for my 42 years. Maybe I got my grandmother's Slavic skin genes. Even at 80, my grandmother's skin hung wrinkle-free from her jowls. Her eyes sunk in puffy pillows of soft cheeks that my little skinny girl face would sink into when she kissed me. Sometimes she grabbed my cheek and pinched it hard while emitting a screech in Slovak.

My skin didn't reflect abuse like I imagined I saw on Marguerite's face. I absorbed it rather than let it leave visible scars.

Eric never hit me. He even showed up at 6:30 in the morning three times a week to paddle next to me while I swam the buoys at Ledbetter Beach to train for the triathlon, a little more than a year ago. He armed himself with a GPS device and a cell phone to call 911 to save me from a highly improbable shark attack. He wielded a pole to hit the shark on the nose if it came too close to me while I swam through the early morning dark ocean water.

The night before one of my practice swims, he told me he wanted to date other women. I showed up at the beach the next morning anyway, exhausted from being awake all night, in despair that he didn't love me.

I pulled on my wetsuit and waded through the kelp, watching the water level rise slowly against my rubber-clad body. He paddled out next to me but his shiny red kayak no longer felt like protection. I put on my goggles, dove into a breaking wave, and started to pull myself through the cold, green murky water. I could only see my hands as each one reached out into the opaque void. I pulled past the first white buoy, lifted my head quickly to locate the next one, breathing in. I put my face back into the water, breathing out. I saw shadows and movement below me. Monsters.

I stopped swimming and pulled off my goggles. My heart beat fast and hard. Salty tears cut through the fishy salt of the ocean water on my mouth. I was petrified.

"I'm getting out," I yelled to Eric through a sob.

"Keep swimming!" Eric commanded, sitting high in his kayak while I treaded water next to it to keep afloat.

"I'm scared," I cried.

"There's nothing down there - it's all in your head."

"You come in here with me and see how scary it is!"

He looked at me and said nothing. The skin around his brown eyes looked lined and tired. I put my goggles back on over my hot eyes, turned away and headed toward the beach. I loved him - why didn't he love me?

I would have wanted Marguerite's job too if I had to contend for a spot in the cloisters. Washing out the dirt, making it all clean again, over and over.

Sister Jeanne continued with the roster of nuns. Sister Josephine: "Prieure", or the Mother Superior. Sister Jeanne didn't describe this job. Perhaps she assumed that Maryam and I already knew what a Mother Superior did. Irene told me that Sister Josephine sometimes yelled at Sister Jeanne.

Sister Jeanne then described her own job as "hotelière": managing the retreat center, the convent's revenue source.

She told us that the convent was poor. "The large donations that used to come from wealthy individuals and families in the community have stopped," she explained. "There's no longer any money coming from the Catholic Church to support our community either; we have to find a way to support ourselves."

I wasn't surprised to hear that the patriarchal Catholic Church had left these women to fend for themselves while giving its priests nice retirement packages. What was I doing here, participating in this misogynistic and oppressive institution? I wondered if these women felt they had been abandoned by the Church.

And we "jeunes filles au pair", or guest workers, also supported this system: our free labor kept the guests' rooms clean, the dining room tables set, cleared and reset, and the guests served their three meals a day.

Our labor also allowed the nuns the time to be who they were: Contemplatives. Prayer was essential to their lives.

Though they all worked to keep the convent solvent by offering religious retreats and housing to paying guests, they disappeared into their cloister every Thursday for "jour de désert" or "day in the desert".

I was attracted by this simple model: work and contemplation. Would it be enough? What about sex, money, friends? Where did they put those desires? I felt imprisoned by my need for distraction. Hey, sailor, come over and look at me!

I had come to this convent to find what they had: something bigger than the distractions of secular life and my desires. Was Jesus this something? The nuns seemed to have it figured out; they were set.

Maybe following "The Rules" for one month in this place where a dozen women spent their days in contemplation and prayer would give me the answer.

"Voilà," Sister Jeanne chirped, and stood up with energy. Our initiation was over. No time for questions; she had to run to welcome guests arriving from Lyon.

After she left, Maryam leaned forward over the color-splotched table, propped up on her elbows. "Do you want to walk down to Intermarché? I want to buy some chocolate." Her face lit up, brown eyes wide and smiling.

I laughed. "No chocolate at the convent during Lent – all we get for dessert is brie and kiwi fruit!"

When I booked my convent sabbatical for the month of April, I wasn't aware that this month was Lent, the most important and most restrictive time in the Catholic liturgical calendar. In a few short weeks, we'd be celebrating the

Resurrection of Jesus but for now, we had to suffer: no dessert.

The Intermarché supermarket was the only source of food within walking distance - other than the three daily meals at the convent. Intermarché was a two-kilometer walk from the convent, past the tiny town of Saint Mathieu de Tréviers. Yesterday I had stocked up on three bottles of the local red Faugères wine and a white Picpoul de Pinet. I hoped they were better than the uneven local table wine that was stored in huge plastic containers in the kitchen that we were served every day at lunch and dinner. I had also combed the supermarket's long aisle of chocolate to find a 6-pack of Suchard Rochers Noirs, my favorite French candy. I couldn't resist these bonbons, each perfect orb wrapped in gold paper. There was nothing in the U.S. that even approximated the dark chocolate nougat coated in toasted hazelnuts.

I didn't need anything, but I followed Maryam's shiny head of bouncing brown hair down the stairs, out of the building and into the bright afternoon sun, away from the Artist's Room, away from the convent. The clean fresh scent of lavender hung in the warm air as we walked toward the yellow mustard field, far in the distance, down the hill to the supermarket that sat below the convent. We walked toward chocolate and away from Sister Jeanne's lists and Lent's Rules.

CHAPTER 8

LINENS

Irene and Agnes and I were assigned to clean three guest rooms on Friday morning but we'd forgotten to pick up clean bed linens when we set out earlier that morning with our buckets and cleaning supplies. I volunteered to fetch them, happy for the opportunity to get outside in the morning sun and walk the quiet convent grounds. I breathed in the cool spring air and walked straight and tall toward the convent's main building. The linen room sat in the far end of the building, near the ravine that bordered the convent property.

The room smelled like starch and hot water, spit for years from Sister Marie-Louise's ancient industrial iron. An old heavy built-in sewing machine cabinet sat in front of a long horizontal window that looked out over the gravel driveway. Out of curiosity, I opened drawers bulging with small spools of thread in red, yellow, bright blue and muted olives, browns, and ochre, a treasure chest of color. Large wooden armoires lined the walls, stuffed with the linens. I opened a tall door to select bedsheets for the three beds that guests had just stripped of their soiled linens.

Each sheet, pillowcase, towel, washcloth and rag at the convent was marked with a symbol that a nun had sewn by hand into the right bottom corner of the fabric. "Torchons" were used in the kitchen and a V had been stitched with red thread for Vaisselle, or kitchen. "Serviettes", a word I thought translated as napkin, were embroidered with a red lumpy M for mains, or hands. Since these two pieces of cloth looked identical, only the M or V found in the corner distinguished their specific and different uses but I couldn't sort out the difference – I just knew there was an important difference that needed to be respected. The symbol also determined which hook each linen would be hung from over a sink. The stitching was bumpy and crudely finished as though the woman who stitched had been assigned the job as punishment, or by someone who was blind.

The symbols also served to segregate the linens into guest linens, linens for the "jeune filles au pair", and rags. The "jeune filles au pair" linens were thin and worn. This system was familiar to me, where guests are treated differently than family.

Since leaving my mother's system of laundry and linens 25 years ago, I had progressively altered her method. In my own home, I kept a hierarchy of linens as my mother did: thin washcloths with frayed borders sat in a pile next to cheery white and yellow ones, some whose tags I hadn't yet removed.

In my late 20s, I worked fulltime for the State of Minnesota and made more money than I needed to support my frugal lifestyle. The cash infusion had me forget the rules I was raised with and I strayed. I purchased a set of pale dusty pink German cotton sheets with a raised pattern, luxuriously soft and light, on sale at Dayton's in downtown Minneapolis. They were beautiful, almost luminescent. I had spent $80 for the set and called my mother to share my amazing find. She was shocked. 50/50 cotton/poly sheets at a tenth of the price were expensive enough; what was I thinking?

I ran my hand over the pile of thin convent linens, soft and faded to yellow. I remembered being wrapped together with Eric in creamy Swiss linens and the warm smell of his smooth olive skin.

My former lover kept no hierarchy of linens; all his linens were the finest quality. When he was my guest, I sought to emulate this equality of linens. His visits forced me to purchase linens that would express what I wanted him to know about me: bright, cute, sunny, and new, someone without the secret clinging to a hierarchical hypothesis about the world and herself.

Our relationship began when he invited me to go camping with him and his friends in Big Sur. We shared a tent and talked all night. The next morning, he told me he saw our yet-to-be-born son in a dream. That sealed the deal – I was caught. I invited Eric to my best friend's wedding in Ojai. I was in love with him; he seemed smitten too – people told me. He said he hated weddings but he went with me anyway. He told me he didn't dance but we danced together all night.

In four months, it was over. Maybe I should have been more patient, given him more time. I missed looking into his rich brown eyes, the weight of his bulk on top of me.

I knew his priorities: work and golf. He made no promises - ever. He would kiss me quickly and rush to his big black BMW, saying only good-bye. No plans, no next time. An Olympic figure skater with perfect jumps and twirls, executed with clean beauty.

Men knew how to work me. Push this button (expensive bottle of wine and lobster in truffle sauce) and you'll get my attention. Push this one (suddenly pull me against you while we walk on State Street and kiss me hard and long in the cold night) and I'll put you up for the night. And another: don't say too much, just enough to make me analyze its meaning all week. Look at me, down at me, from your tall dark beauty, the warm toasted scent of a cologne tucking me in whose name I thought I'd never forget. Are those Audubons on the wall of your hyper-contemporary house in the hills?

I would compose an email and save it until the right time came to send it, as a prompt - I'm still here. Call me. His voice on the phone played with my eardrum - aural sex. I could still hear it, a voice that feels like falling into happy inebriation, rolling on fine sheets in a big bed.

I needed too much. Instead, I should settle. Grow where you're planted, some advised. To those who recommended this type of gardening, I would have said to them, go throw-up.

The convent was supposed to act as an antidote for these desires that made me crazy. Instead, the convent aggravated them. During my free time, I thought about Eric, about the others, about another who might come along and rescue me with designer clothes and weekend trips to Los Angeles when I got back to Santa Barbara.

Was it wrong to want a man who could take care of me? One who made me feel adored? I was here in this convent, had taken a vow of sexual poverty, like these Dominican nuns had, and though voluntarily, it was only for a month.

But I wasn't a nun. I just lived like one, until someone came along to distract me. I looked at the celadon green Chinese robe I bought at Franck et Fils in Paris, my one hold-out from plunging wholly into this month of deprivation. I wasn't going to get rid of it or even hide it away in a drawer. It draped casually over the little wooden desk chair, waiting until tomorrow afternoon's ritual when I put it on after a morning of maid's work, lunch and a shower. Then I'd make myself a cup of Lapsong Souchong tea that I'd purchased at the Hédiard store in Paris, stir in some milk, and sit on my narrow bed, thinking about what I should do with my life after I left this convent.

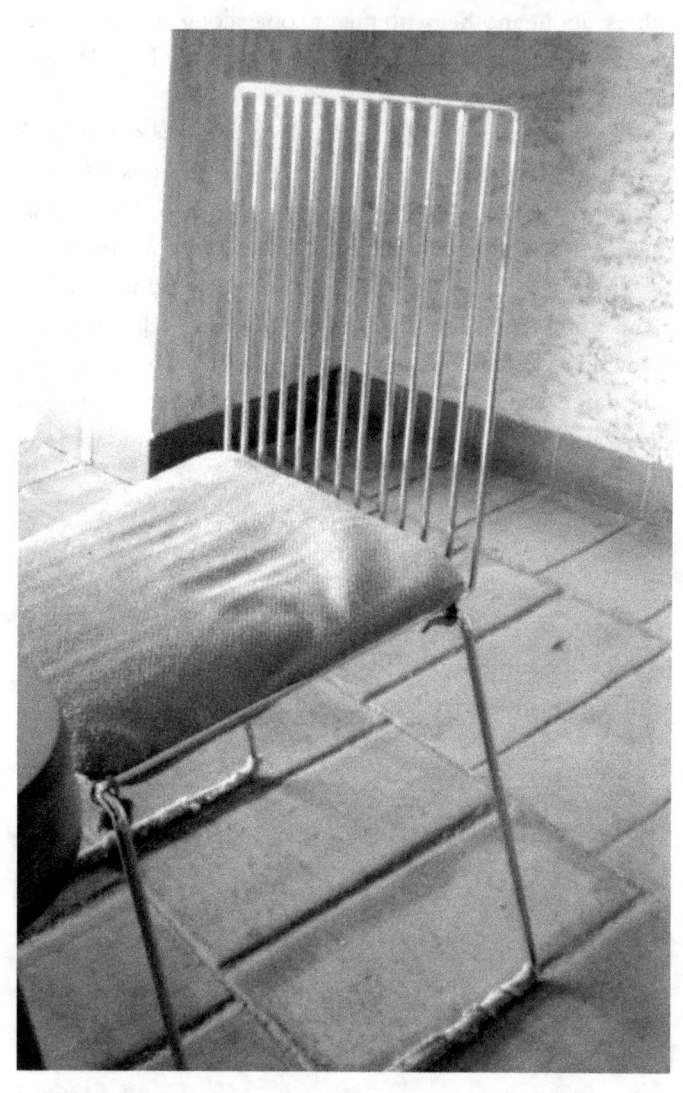

CHAPTER 9

THEOLOGY

A young Jesuit priest visited the convent to deliver a Lenten lecture on Stoicism. Agnes, my Czech co-worker, sat next to me, both of us in chairs with little tables attached. She still wore her blue maid's apron; I had taken mine off before we entered the conference room.

We had raced through preparing three guest rooms so that we could attend this event. Sister Jeanne told us at our work meeting that the speaker was a very important theological scholar. I hoped for some intellectual stimulation.

Agnes leaned forward, her chin in her hand, hair chopped short like a novice's: a nun-in-training. Her short black hair and white skin drew out the green in her gray eyes. Her perpetual white smile made me wonder what she was thinking.

Was she a real Catholic, a believer? Me, I was here for the quiet. I had already done my time as a Catholic growing up in suburban Minneapolis: confession every Saturday afternoon, the rosary every night during Lent, and Wednesday night Catechism classes after school. And I had a major credential too: my uncle was a priest. I could take anyone with my pedigree.

One Spring Break in junior high, my family piled into the station wagon with the tent and sleeping bags and drove to visit Mother Seton's National Shrine near Baltimore. My mother considered her my patron saint since we shared the same name – Elizabeth Ann – and she was also American. The only memory of that pilgrimage was my brother falling into the creek at the shrine. One summer, my family camped for several weeks through Canada (different station wagon) with a stop at the Shrine of Saint Anne de Beaupré in Quebec. I walked up steep wooden stairs on my knees to reach a box of her bones. I don't remember my siblings joining me for that painful ritual.

But that was ancient history. I was now curious about the contemplative life that religious nuns and monks lived. But joining the Church – or rejoining in my case - came with a price: having to listen to guys like the one in front of me.

The Jesuit led with sin – a good hook. "The consequence of sin is the loss of one's freedom." He delivered his text with dry arrogance through black, half-closed eyes. His skinny angular body sat comfortably in a blue pullover and jeans. I sensed he considered his presence a gift to this country convent. He spoke slowly in perfectly-enunciated French. His black hair was flattened to one side of his face and I wondered when he had last bathed. What an asshole.

Confessor, tell us how bad we are and then tell us that only you, and men like you with advanced degrees in theology, hold the keys to our freedom. That sin will cost us ten Hail Marys and a lifelong belief that we're damned.

Celibates surrounded me, sitting low in the little desks, earnestly taking notes as he listed the cardinal virtues – or did he say pleasures? When he compared the New Age movement to Stoicism, his face moved away from his notes as though they stunk of feces. Then he dismissed Buddhism, a religion more ancient than his.

The Jesuit gestured confidently like the master of all knowledge. "The Stoics separate God and the world; for Christians, God and the world are the same," he said, lifting his chin.

Who was he to assume such superiority? The plastic chairs were hard and my body felt bloated, too small for the chair. My face felt warm and I started to sweat. I was female, still fertile, sitting with women who hadn't had sex ever, whose bodies were only used to carry their souls around. I imagined the Jesuit's bad breath, the sour kind that emanated from a stomach that eats at itself because it has nothing in it.

The room was quiet but alive; this man must have been important to get such attention. I took notes too, on brown, thin paper, so thin that the pen sank into the pad, imprinting the sheets below.

Talk about God and Jesus being one and God made flesh made me squirm. But the Jesuit believed it - these nuns did too. They listened rapturously to the wisdom emanating from this boy priest who delivered a truth that only one endowed with male genitalia is allowed to speak. I looked over at Sister Dominique, old, small and energetically upright, and Sister Patrice, old, small, and bent, both generously attentive from their little chairs. Both women were probably as educated as he was but their gender rendered them theologically impotent to speak with his arrogant and blessed authority.

He continued, delivering his sermon: Christianity made God incarnate, or human. This was scandalous for the Jews and craziness to the pagans, the boyish priest explained. God is transcendent in Judaism. I stopped paying attention.

Jews. Now I was really pissed. Eric was haunting me, even in this bastion of Catholicism.

The boy priest closed his notes in a book; the lecture was over. My body felt leaden and trapped in my small desk. I watched the full room empty slowly.

Did my Jewish ex-lover know that his belief in God's transcendence and mine in the Holy Trinity would eventually doom our relationship? I doubt he knew the meaning of transcendence; he couldn't even explain to me the significance of his High Holidays.

We never argued about religion or even discussed it. Though he was Jewish and I was not, he told me that he was open to a relationship, even marriage, with a woman who wasn't Jewish. But four months later, he sat on the edge of my sofa, apologizing, maybe, that my willingness to convert to Judaism wouldn't be enough: I had to have been born Jewish. I screamed at him while he stood in my doorway, head bowed, on his way out. I imagined I was not the first woman to unleash rage over this act. He had lied for months and I knew it the whole time.

I wanted to believe I was wrong about him. I didn't listen when the evidence was presented: on his trips to New York, he saw his friend Lynn, a woman he grew up with in Queens. He showed me pictures of Lynn, dark-haired and smiling, while I unwrapped presents he brought me, his stomach full of his mother's babka. So what kind of friend was she, I wanted to ask? But I didn't want to know.

I wanted him to express his love, not his doubt.

Two months later, still crushed from Eric's rejection, I took my mother with me to Rome. It was New Year's Day when we landed. A cult in Colorado had just declared that it would bomb Jerusalem for the millennium's sake.

Our Roman guidebook recommended visiting the synagogue near the Trastevere neighborhood to see its beautiful interior. My mother and I walked up to the armed soldier in front of the synagogue. Could we enter? No, his head motioned. We turned to watch a dark-haired young woman pull a little boy up the temple's stone stairs, push open a door and disappear into the cavernous building. I argued with the man who answered my knocks on that same door. I wanted in. He shut the door without responding.

Trastevere was getting dark. The streets behind the synagogue were lit by yellow shop windows that displayed the poppy seed and prune pastries that my Slovak grandmother made in her sunny floral Minneapolis kitchen when I was a little girl. I entered a crowded and loud bakery with Hebrew painted like graffiti on the fogged windows. I stood pale and blonde in the middle of dark women and men, separate and silent, treading in the stew of their unfamiliar and sharp language, defiantly not of their tribe.

I had come to Rome in search of an old, benign Catholicism, hoping to heal my broken heart but also in reaction to almost jumping ship from the Mother Church. I wondered if it was time to reconsider Catholicism; I had definitely fallen far away from the One True Faith over the past 20 years.

To stew in it again, I left my mother to nap at the hotel while I wandered under the frescoed ceilings of the Vatican, visually drowning in blues and greens and yellows. Every evening, my mother and I sat in a different magnificent Roman church listening to a choir or string quartet, breathing in the incense burned at a Mass two hours earlier.

Out of curiosity, we entered the Office for the Propagation for the Faith. The name read like Monty Python movie material. Inside, we walked through the clinical foyer, toward the sentry in a glass box in dark undertaker's clothes. His dead eyes refused our questions and I sensed disease under his powdered gray pallor. I felt dirty, a medieval wench in smelly rags. The Church's glorification of masculine power, and dismissal of female anything, seemed sexually perverted, more than any pornography. Popes elevated on gilded thrones, seated above Mary Magdalene and her unworthy sisters, watching them writhe in eternal damnation for the sin of femininity. After two days of prowling through cathedrals and basilicas, I felt physically ill.

We ended our pilgrimage of Catholicism and spent more time in cafés. We sat until noon in the hotel's pale green and yellow breakfast room whose windows presented a view of rooftops dotted with ancient statues that watched over Rome. The young server, whose haircut suggested he might be a skinhead, stared at me while he refilled the samovar with hot tea.

We sat outside at night in cafés heated by lamps, watching beautiful Romans gesture over their coffees. Some of them looked like Eric. My mother noticed that some of them looked at me. But I was here as penance, my mother on my arm.

I didn't tell my mother about Eric, not the details. She never seemed very interested in who I was dating and when she did inquire about a new one, she always got the name wrong. "How's Mike?" she'd ask. It's Matt, mom.

We sat in a crowded café, facing a vase of fresh pink and yellow tulips on a lacquered piano of mahogany late on a cold afternoon. I asked my mother to recount the story of Aunt Rita, my great aunt and my mother's namesake. She sailed to Europe in the 1920s and also worked several years as a schoolteacher. She fell in love with a Lutheran, a mortal sin in my mother's Irish Catholic family. The relationship ended but my mother was scant on details so I suspected it was ugly.

Was it easier to stick with one's kind, not to stray? I had dated only one Catholic seriously, though neither of us was serious about the religion we'd been raised in. I had dated several Jewish men and a couple of Muslims too, along with men from various Protestant sects who didn't seem too interested in their religious identity. The Church felt like a family member I didn't really like but couldn't get rid of.

The next day, on Piazza Farnese, we found a convent full of women who follow Saint Birgitta, the patron saint of Sweden. A black nun in soft dove gray fabric bustled around us excitedly, while her fellow gray-clad sisters, crowing like a bevy of pigeons, lead us to Saint Birgitta's bones, enclosed in a tomb which sat in a silent room of heavy stained glass windows and dark blue velvet upholstered chairs. The nuns were African, revering a Swedish saint and living in Rome.

They smiled without stopping and invited us to stay for Mass.

The Saint Birgitta nuns in Rome pushed no theology, forced no choice between Judaism and Catholicism, but accepted me, even welcomed me.

The convent in rural Languedoc wasn't turning out to be the realization of dream I'd had. I didn't sign up to be lectured to by a celibate theologian who spouted the same perverted Papal theology my mother and I were assaulted with in Rome. Instead of offering rescue for my drowned soul, I felt pushed against the wall with the hard-core Catholicism the Jesuit spouted. I didn't want to be forced to choose. I wouldn't twist myself to satisfy their rules.

In the bright conference room, the little chairs with their attached desk tables, now empty, faced alertly toward the front of the room. What was I getting out of these bizarre lectures? Certainly no clarity! I wanted this month to explore who I was and what I believed. The convent promised to give me space to "reprendre souffle", space to breathe and reflect. I wanted it to be the right place.

But instead of finding what I wanted and discovering who I was, I was resurrecting old anger and arguments I'd had with Catholic theology since I was in high school. I was 42 now. I thought I had left this all behind decades ago. But here I was, living in one of its institutions.

PART II

CHAPTER 10

STEPHAN / IRENE

Irene stopped to catch her breath on our climb to "the ruin", at the end of a trail of limestone and granite and fragrant sage. She had switched her regularly scheduled Thursday afternoon French lesson to another day so that we could take advantage of the perfect weather. Yesterday, the sky was dark with thick clouds and linear patches of gray, like the matted fur of a cat that picks fights frequently. The wind was constant in this Herault region and created dramatic and changeable skies.

She smiled impishly and her blue eyes sparkled but she didn't look at me. Her small round face turned a little red. "Stephan and I watched TV in the convent lounge last night," she started. "We drank tea and ate chocolate."

"Oh?" I asked. I wanted to know more but didn't want to push. I knew she had a crush on Stephan.

At the convent, a male person was either a priest or monk or husband of a couple who stayed at the convent on retreat. There was one exception: Stephan. He was Sister Jeanne's nephew – 20 years old, Belgian, dark, tall, thin and likable. Warm dark pupils bobbed slowly in the whites of his eyes, droopy with future attractiveness. He studied agricultural economics at the university and was at the convent to prepare for his biology exams. Like us female au pairs, he had to work mornings for his room and board.

One evening, Stephan gathered us in the TV room to watch his favorite film on video, *Les Visiteurs*. I recognized the actor, Jean Reno, but couldn't understand the French dialogue. He stopped the tape frequently to explain the cultural references that don't exist in the United States. "Here he's making a play on words about the French aristocracy, the lesser nobles," Stephan explained. He laughed riotously. I wanted to understand but couldn't. "And this part, this is about an historical event from the thirteenth century between two poets...that decided X...." What? So many layers from so much education and history.

I saw him on the convent grounds with Cedric the Handyman, carrying tools or a pail. He was lucky - he got to do men's work, outside, no chemicals.

Irene liked Stephan. I liked Stephan.

Last week, Stephan found me in the recreation room, mopping the floor, to tell me that the American stock market was crashing. "There's a copy of the *Le Monde* newspaper in the convent library to explain what's happening." I felt so isolated in the convent, totally removed from the financial world to which I had once paid attention. This news seemed from another time.

He littered his French with Americanisms – crash, wow, OK, cool. I watched his mouth, trying to keep up. His lazy brown eyes contrasted with his hyperactive speech, a crooked smile in his long face. He was the only person I met at the convent who registered any positive reaction to my culture.

At the breakfast table that morning, my grapefruit squirted Jean-Pierre, the convent chef, in the face. "Ack, le Scud du Clinton!" he squealed – something about Clinton's Scud missile hitting him. Tiny animated man with a huge nose and forehead and no butt - almost a French caricature.

At lunch, Cedric the Handyman sat erect at the head of the table, diagonally from me.

The sun hit him sideways and his very large nose cast a fuzzy shadow across his long face. He had big teeth, a dark widow's peak and cheeks with hollows. He constantly corrected my pronunciation which annoyed me because Agnes's pronunciation was worse - her Czech accent flavored all her vowels. He never corrected her. I felt picked on the most, for bad pronunciation and for being from the U.S., home of obese people who eat at McDonald's, drink Coke, and put sauce on everything.

I knew my presence at the convent doing menial labor confused Cedric the Handyman. He told me assuredly that Americans always hire someone to do their dirty work. I enjoyed spearing Cedric's confident assumptions about me, the American. As my country's representative at the convent, I maintained a cheery disposition no matter what anyone threw at me. When Sister Jeanne asked me to pick up a guest at the bus stop in town two days earlier, she gave me the keys to the noisy little white Peugeot. Cedric stood in the middle of the driveway with his big feet splayed, large hands on his narrow hips and watched me back down the steep and long driveway in reverse, down to the main road. Later at lunch that day, he declared that Americans don't know how to operate manual transmissions and that in fact, they don't even exist in the United States. He delivered his declaration with his long and large French nose raised high, punctuating his certainty with his fork.

I was fascinated by Cedric's and the others' reaction to me, but I was a strange representative of American culture. I didn't eat fast food very often and didn't watch TV. But I wanted to hear more, ask questions, but I feared they would hear my questions as defensive.

Stephan didn't trash the U.S., make jokes about Americans, say how stupid we were, that we didn't understand history, and couldn't drive manual transmission cars. Instead, at lunch each day, he taught me a slang phrase which I put on my laptop's screen saver as a way to remember it.

Stephan saw that I was more than what I appeared to be at that moment, standing with a mop in my hand, in a blue apron and stretched-out black leggings. I wanted a man like Stephan.

Irene was like Stephan – open, curious, and smart. They were young – the future of Europe – a new generation, one that didn't feel inferior to the U.S. and didn't feel threatened by American culture.

I didn't want to lose them to the banality of romance. Irene would become obsessed, as she had been with an older man she dated back in Norway. "It's over with him," she told me, but his birthday was approaching and she wanted to send him a card. Should she write a note to express anything more than "Happy Birthday"?

I hoped she wouldn't emulate the pattern my romantic journey had taken. When I wanted to follow a dream or passion, I thwarted the plan by drowning myself in a relationship. I used men, unconsciously, to avoid being true to myself. I gave up myself, little pieces at a time.

When I finally broke it off, I felt relief. I could fill my lungs to full capacity again.

Ten years ago, I met John, a major league baseball fanatic and major beer drinker. We began a friendship by playing tennis in Loring Park in Minneapolis then would spend the rest of the evening at a bar on Hennepin Avenue, drinking pints of beer and talking about the theatre. After nine months, I could consume a six-pack of Bud Lite or Pabst Blue Ribbon in an evening, sitting in front of his television watching football. In those nine months, we never left the Twin Cities metropolitan area, only once venturing into Saint Paul, to my apartment, less than ten miles away.

I was plastic, conforming almost gratefully to his habits and activities. I didn't care about what I was doing with my life; he was a good excuse not to.

I didn't want Irene to wander aimlessly through this tangled romantic landscape. I wanted her to follow her dreams, not trade them in for sex, the disguise of true love.

Irene told me that when she met a boy she liked, she threw her arms around him. Her friends tried to restrain her, this desperate behavior, trapping a man in your arms, claiming him. I imagined her small, cherubic freckled face beaming puppy-love into his. Because she was little, I imagined she stood on her toes and reached her round body, squeezed into tight corduroy jeans, up and against the boy, her shiny white-blonde hair grazing her buttocks. Or maybe she'd wear a miniskirt, which she didn't wear on the convent grounds, only in Montpellier, also tight, revealing her short, muscular white legs.

She started real life young, a healthy, welcoming, fearless embrace of it. She didn't negotiate the barrier, analyze the barrier, and talk herself into climbing over it and joining those on the other side to enjoy each other. The nuns accused her of being coquettish. She took risks - like Stephan.

At 19, I was plump like Irene, blonde, interested in the world, and interested in talking about it. The intellectual connection felt more profound than the sexual one.

Then I lost my plumpness. I met a boy in college and we talked into the night about opera, listening to records on his turntable and analyzing the music's layering of poetry and sound.

After a few dates, his intellectual interest in me soured into a sexual one. The pump didn't yield any more, not even after I traded a little skin for some more talking. Once the sexual pact had been made, I changed. He did too. I was no longer a brainy young woman but a sexual one. I had stepped down a rung. The body always seemed to trump the mind.

Oh, isn't she cute, another lover said to a table of his friends at a bar. I was excited, animated, wrapped up in telling a story. They all laughed. I hit him.

When I was 14, my father told me to hold off on dating until I had finished graduate school. He warned me away from what his wife had become: dependent. Initially, he was attracted to her independent 1950s "Sex and the Single Girl" life on Girard Avenue in Minneapolis. Four women living together, in their early 30s, all single. Then she married him, had four kids, and found herself dependent – stuck in the suburbs for almost 50 years.

My mother, the intellectual, left that world when she married. Kids, suburbs, bridge club. Who can keep it up? So instead of reading Kierkegaard, she chopped vegetables. She defended her hours of chopping, proud that we were the only kids that ate real food in the fast-food sixties.

I didn't want to be a housewife but I didn't want to be a sex object either. Even Marlo Thomas, my idol, seemed to have to choose between these two roles as "That Girl", a show I watched religiously. I'd had more than a taste of being a sex object at 13, with quickly developing breasts and already rounded hips. When my Uncle Leland and his family visited our house, he greeted me by pressing my body into his protruding belly and telling me I was a sex machine. His actions confused me. It didn't seem right that this old man would say these things and squeeze my buttocks, but no one objected. My dad's response was "Oh, that's just Leland." Leland, the World War II veteran who took shrapnel in the butt, which granted him dispensation for any behavior. Once, I protested by refusing to leave my room when he and his family came over for dinner. My mother angrily told me my behavior was impolite so I conceded. Uncle Leland had gone for her too.

At 16, I marched in support of the Equal Rights Amendment through downtown Minneapolis and learned a new phrase: Male Chauvinist Pig.

Soon after, at a family get-together on a Sunday after Mass, he came after me. I was at the end of his line-up, after my mother. As he approached, his big pudgy body coming in for my expanding adolescent one, like a bird flying unexpectedly from my throat, I yelled "Get your hands off me, you Male Chauvinist Pig!"

That was the last get-together with that family.

When I discovered sex at 20, it was so easy, and I liked it. I was seduced by the attention I got. I feared Irene was like me.

But Irene had a life ahead of her, like I did at 19. Ignore that handsome man in the corner! Go forth and conquer! Change the world with your energy and passion! Don't fall into the mundane activities of love, marriage and reproduction.

When I was 19, I stayed behind in Paris after my semester abroad at the Institute Catholique ended, while my fellow students returned to Minnesota to finish out the academic year. My classmate David stayed behind too. We were both enrolled in the same "Semester Abroad in Paris" program but he attended a different Catholic college back in Minnesota, Saint Mary's College, the brother school to Saint Teresa's, my women's Catholic college. He was tall and handsome, relaxed in his body like a swimmer who had just finished working out. He wasn't interested in me; I couldn't imagine he would have been. I was shy, plump and introverted, battered by my mother's attempts to put me on a diet throughout my teenage years. Until I was thin, he wouldn't be interested.

Some days, David and I wandered around grey Paris together. We purchased small black-shelled mussels from the market on Rue Mouffetard and steamed them in butter and dry white burgundy, squeezed together in his small kitchen nook in the studio apartment he rented. The warm sweet butter overwhelmed the cold dank odors from the apartment's ancient walls. Had I been Irene, I would have thrown my arms around him, this handsome young man in blue jeans and a grey sweatshirt emblazoned with the name of his American college.

But I was too shy. I still had the stain of religion on me. I scorned my fellow students who told me they had "met" guys while traveling on the Eurailpass through Western Europe that semester. But I was jealous - and curious too. How did they do it? It was a mystery to me - how one went about engaging with a man.

My first kiss had occurred a year earlier, in my freshman year of college, on the floor in an empty dark room in a dormitory building in Madison. I was visiting my best friend from high school who instead of enrolling in a women's Catholic college in rural Minnesota, had enrolled at the University in Madison and had a sex date with one of the guys in her dorm every Friday at 3:00 P.M. On Friday night, a bunch of us watched a film in someone's room that starred naked women having sex with dogs. The screen was bright blue and German Shepherds panted over the women's pale white bodies. On Saturday night, my roommate lent me some clothes and did my makeup. At her dorm party, I drank several glasses of red mystery punch from the tubs. Then I was on the floor in a dark room, rolling around with a cute boy and lost in the ecstatic pleasure of our lips touching. He stopped kissing me and said he'd be right back. I got up off the floor, wandered out of the room to find my friend, dazed and happy and drunk.

These experiences were nothing like any I was having at the College of Saint Teresa.

My grandmother and mother had both attended Saint Teresa's; my grandmother studied there in 1917, and my mother graduated from this women's college at the end of World War II. It was named for Saint Teresa of Avila, a Spanish mystic saint. The campus sat near the Mississippi River and from my dormitory window, I could see the limestone bluffs that walled the west side of the water. The campus' brown brick buildings, topped with orange Mediterranean ceramic roof tiles, recalled Avila, Spain.

I attended for one year, my freshman year of college. The nuns wore knee-length habits, managed the college and taught courses along with secular faculty members. It was an experience rich in academic rigor.

The classes were small and my professors nurtured my intellectual curiosity and supported my efforts to develop my intellectual interests. The astronomy course included a 2:00 A.M. class meeting on the lawn outside my dormitory to view the stars. The professor lived a block away. My political science professor took a group of us dancing at the Holiday Inn on the main highway that went north to Minneapolis and south to Iowa. He taught us the foxtrot. Other than the smelly downtown bars filled with old drunks, this hotel lounge was the only evening entertainment available in the small town of Winona.

The nuns' lives were peripheral to my experience at the College of Saint Teresa. However, my work-study job at the college switchboard was managed by Sister Mary, an old craggy-faced nun in a black habit. And once I argued with the financial aid nun about the paltry sum of money the college offered against the tuition bill. If I was out after midnight on a Saturday night (not allowed to freshmen until the second semester), I had to enter the freshman dormitory through a musty underground tunnel from the upperclassmen's dormitory, checking in with the nun standing guard at the entrance to the tunnel.

Being a student at the Institute Catholique a year later didn't come with the same constraints I was under at Saint Teresa's but I still couldn't act, even when I fell in love with another man in Paris that semester, a French one. He was a graduate student of American history, studying at one of the Paris university campuses on the city's periphery. He lent me his books and ideas for crafting my essay for the Truman Scholarship which had a fast-approaching deadline. I sat on his bed, alarmed by the marijuana stench, imagining depraved acts by two people struggling under heavy blankets in this cold dorm room. He offered me lukewarm mint tea and one of his cigarettes.

He paced the small room, talking about President Truman, looking one-hundred percent French: tight blue jeans and a blue wool pullover sweater, with masses of curly red-brown hair. I listened and took notes, refusing to remove my Navy pea coat. I wanted something to happen with this brilliant French man but I wasn't like Irene at 19.

At the ruin on the top of Saint Loup Peak, I asked Irene how last night went with Stephan. "Stephan is not a man but a boy, only interested in boy's things, not me," she sighed. So Stephan was a boy: he lived in the realm of the mind, wanting to connect in that room, not the bedroom.

I was relieved - I didn't want to lose her to him. I didn't want to lose Stephan either.

CHAPTER 11

MONTPELLIER

On my first designated day off from convent work, which occurred every Tuesday, I got up early, before breakfast. In the cool silence, the low sun stealthily illuminated the black vineyards like a searchlight, exposing newly sprouted bright green leaves. I wanted to catch the first bus that left at 6:35 A.M. from a parking lot in downtown Saint Mathieu de Tréviers to the train station in Montpellier. I quickly dressed in clothes that I didn't wear at the convent: a dark blue long broomstick skirt with black tights and black flat Italian shoes, and a wool sweater with large pearl buttons. I rimmed my eyes with liner and mascara.

I was late leaving my room at the convent so jogged down the dirt road that lead from the convent into Saint Mathieu where the bus from the town north stopped. I heard a car behind me in the dawn light so moved to the right. I could hear it slow next to me, its motor buzzing like a wind-up toy. "Bonjour, Mademoiselle!" the driver called out. "Are you going into Montpellier?" he asked. "Would you like a ride?"

Panting heavily, I got in the front seat of the little blue car, amazed at my good fortune. Riding with him instead of the bus would cut almost one hour off the 20 kilometer trip.

The driver lived in one of the new, large well-built houses near the convent and worked at the university in Montpellier. I spoke French with this little man in his little blue car and was incredulous that the words came out of my mouth so easily. I rarely spoke with someone for a sustained amount of time. Most French at the convent was conveyed in short messages and received directions. But this was a real conversation and I was ready with the language to participate.

The words willingly emerged from storage, released from their original acquisition 25 years ago when I studied French, my major in college. Well-constructed French sentences flowed out of me like birdsong as we circled the many roundabouts on the way south into Montpellier.

He had worked at the university for a long time, hence the big well-built house. This was his commute, just like a commute in the U.S. But it looked and felt different - it was a French commute. After fifteen round-a-bouts, he turned sharply into a parking lot at the university and parked next to a building of stone, dark from layers of dirt. I could smell the moldy rich moisture the lichen held. The sun was bright at 7:00 A.M. and I remembered that I was in the Mediterranean.

Irene had lent me a map of Montpellier and a booklet from the chamber of commerce that listed each store and its location. I started at the center of town, at the morning market's fruit and vegetable stalls. The green cabbage leaves under the black-skinned vendors' feet smelled raw and fresh, and I could identify the peppery perfume from the endive and fennel. It was April and the trees were green, not like Paris in March where tulips had sprouted prematurely in the bright green grass next to bare branches. Though it was green in Montpellier, it was still cool enough to wear wool.

Like a deer in the headlights, I struggled with which café to sit at for a cup of tea. The old yellowed one at the end of the square was full of men wearing blue aprons identical to the one I wore while cleaning rooms at the convent. I chose a brightly lit café with white tables and chairs across from a cheese vendor's stall. I sat at a small table near the street.

The black tea arrived in the convent's familiar white café cup and saucer. I felt anonymous and urban and relieved; I had escaped Grandmother's house and was on my grand adventure. I was released from cleaning rooms and toilets, puzzling over which tattered gray rag to use and then puzzling over which pile in the laundry room to deposit the dirty rag on, showing up for lunch at 12:30 sharp to eat overcooked vegetables, chlorinated white bread and if I could stomach it, the gravy-smothered piece of meat. Today I could order a glass of wine for lunch in a restaurant whose menu would give me choices that might include leafy green salads, served with a basket of fresh whole grain bread. Real French cooking, warm and buttery, crisp and colorful. I anticipated my luncheon bistro: I would sit alone, mysterious and unknown, and therefore an interesting quantity in this town.

I paid for the tea and entered the market. Out on the street, I felt uncomfortable; dark men stared. My pale skin and light brown hair marked me as foreign.

Though the convent was boring, it was safe. Within the few of days since I arrived at the convent, I had already secured my existence there. My routine was fixed, dependable. Everyone knew who I was: Elizabeth, the American. Away from the convent, my anonymity felt like a liability.

All the excitement of coming to the big city with several hours of unstructured freedom in front of me suddenly turned into disorientation and indecision. I had a long to-do list and a map, but stood frozen in front of the tantalizing cheese stall which beckoned me to sample the creamy and tangy white chèvre. Instead, I chose a safe start: head for the church.

Saint Roch is the patron saint of the Languedoc area - a noble man who gave it all up for God and almost starved to death but for a dog who delivered a piece of bread to his cave every day. Thus Saint Roch is the patron saint of dogs, as well as diseases and bachelors. The Cathedral was on the map, near the university. I walked through streets pinched narrow with tall stone buildings on both sides. The yellow sun found one side of the street's smooth face, its yellow light warming the old stone, but left the other side hiding in the cool and dark. An alto voice answered another one with a short echo, and both bounced down the twisty corridor, breaking the morning silence.

At the end of the maze was a square full of closed yellow umbrellas, waiting to be opened for lunch, and against the sky, a pointed witch's hat covered in black tiles – the medieval tower of the Cathedral. This was not one of the confectionery churches of Boulanger's Paris; this was motes and chivalry and knights and strong queens. And I had been here before.

I had identified only one past life: Sixteenth-century Prague, Saint Agnes Convent. Ten years earlier, I attended a violin and piano recital at the Saint Agnes Convent in Prague. Before the concert started, I left my alcoholic and soon to be ex-boyfriend sitting in the concert hall to find the bathroom. I walked the convent's corridors, under vaulted ceilings of stone, as I had in the 1500s. I wasn't Czech that evening but did that matter? And today I wasn't French, but I had been here, in this church, on ground that was under French rule in the 1300s, when this church was built.

The empty church felt more like a museum than a place of refuge, but I felt calmed in its quiet space. I looked at the painted canvases on the walls and then checked the bulletin board for local announcements to get an idea of what this community was all about. I saw that I'd miss a choral concert at the church this weekend. I also realized that I was in Saint Pierre's Cathedral, not Saint Roch's. That explained the absence of dog statuary.

Outside the quiet Cathedral, my body felt light in the mid-morning freshness. I entered a square bordered by sandstone buildings and walked past a violin shop, the third one that morning. Someone was testing the instrument and the violin's strings produced a rich amber sound that transported me out of my body and into my soul. The music was like food and I could feel it plump and full.

I left the still square, turned left and boom! I landed on a street with honking cars and shoppers trying to avoid colliding with each other's bodies and bags in the narrow sidewalk. Glass doors were open to the street. I walked into a store selling CDs by African and European artists. Exposure to another collection of life; this was the excitement of foreign travel. More information, data, something new and novel. During career exploration courses I took after finding that the first couple of jobs out of graduate school didn't thrill me, I had tried to identify my desire for the novel as an indicator of a potential career path. Advertising? Design? Travel agent? Nothing fit. Culture monitor? But wasn't everyone excited by the new? No, not so. I had a cousin in southern Minnesota who asked why I liked to go to France so often; he preferred to park his Winnebago next to a stream a mile away from his farm and fish all day. He had fought in the Vietnam War, which may have explained his disinterest in travel. He had already experienced enough exciting foreign travel for a lifetime by dodging bullets.

I had recently discovered Youssour N'Dour, a Senegalese singer. Sister Jeanne had lent us au pairs a videotape of *Kirikou et La Sourcière*, an animated African children's story with Youssour N'Dour's music on its soundtrack. We au pairs watched the videotape again and again for several evenings after dinner in the convent's TV room, lined up in hard chairs at a long cold conference table, seduced by the music's syncopation. Last month in Paris, I walked by a concert hall where hundreds of dark young men with thick frizzy hair and tight jeans stood outside to buy or sell tickets. I didn't know then that this singer was a superstar.

The *Kirikou* soundtrack reopened my fascination with music, and I was surprised again that it could move me, that someone could create something new and appealing after all the music that had already been created. I leaned against the bin of CDs in a small shop and listened to several of N'Dour's tracks on headphones. But the music was too loud, too many starts and stops, his voice harsh. These pieces lacked the rolling syncopation I wanted to seduce me again.

Thin young French men in blue jeans and leather jackets picked through the disks silently, staying only for a short time. They walked in and out, one at a time. They brushed past me, not seeming to notice me even though I was the only female in the store.

In Montpellier, like in Paris, I was desperate to acquire things, French things, so that through their acquisition, I could become French. I wanted to change myself, take on a new identity. Being an American was not interesting, was coarse, too nouveau, and loudly garish. But I was living here now, in a country I had dreamed about since I was a teenager. This was my opportunity to assume French taste and style.

I was white-faced, pale, and curvy, from Slavic and Irish stock. My body wasn't petite and graceful like the French women whose faces didn't move as they hurried through the streets and who smelled so divine in perfumes I didn't know. Jean Seberg cut off her hair and wore stripes to look French in the movie *Breathless*. Otherwise, she too was an American, too sunny, too open, too accessible.

I had developed a bra fetish in Paris when I discovered Princesse Tam Tam, a lingerie boutique that sold matching bra and panty sets, PJs and swim suits. I decided that French brassieres would transform me. The transformation would be subtle - I'd be the only one who would know. I was thrilled that Montpellier had a Princesse Tam Tam store too.

"Bonjour, Madame," sang the ageless Princesse Tam Tam saleswoman as I entered the store. Her perfectly managed hairstyle was straight out of a 1950s women's magazine. I appreciated that her sex appeal stayed on the tastefully seductive side of the lingerie dividing line.

"Bonjour, Madame," I replied as I cautiously entered the small boutique, confronted with matching sets of bras and panties, like Easter eggs crowded together in a basket. Olive green, red, light blue, lavender. Full cup, demi-cup, push up, padded.

I felt a little out of control, almost faint. I breathed steadily. My mind raced as the slim saleswoman selected various styles. What would happen if I bought, let's say, six Princesse Tam Tams? Though I craved the delicious possibility of beauty that would descend upon me wearing these gorgeous soutiens-gorge, or brassieres, I vowed that the fantasy would stay in my head. It wasn't just a question of funds, it was a personal prohibition against excessive sensual pleasure and too much beauty. A gushing, colorful, three-dimensional life, animated by beautiful brassieres, couldn't win over my frugal, pragmatic allegiance to decent living - AKA convent living.

"Voilà, Madame," the efficient saleswoman said as she left me alone with three candidates. I tried the lacy navy number first with its elegantly contrasting black lining. I wanted this beauty to fit. It didn't.

Suddenly the dressing room curtain blew open. Like a lab technician, the saleswoman examined me and the ill-fitting bra. "You need a smaller size," she said.

I put on the smaller bra while she watched. It squeezed my diaphragm; it was too tight.

"Très jolie," she smiled, inspecting the fit. Very pretty. With her assistance, I discovered that it was easy to push breast flesh around after 40 years of age. In contrast, my

American bra had allowed my breasts to hang where they wanted to, without structure or discipline.

"It seems a little tight, it doesn't really fit," I said. I felt deformed. Nothing French fit my American body.

"Mais non," she said, but no "it fits perfectly." She pulled the straps against my back like she was hoisting up a main sail. My breasts landed a couple levels higher than before. But I felt very secure.

"Très jolie," she said again. Very pretty.

"My breasts look weird, too pointy," I told her, feeling out of my league in the brassiere arena.

"Très jolie," she said again. "The bra creates a fine silhouette."

Wearing this bra would certainly create a different silhouette for me. Anyway, I was in France – there was no right way for my breasts to look.

"Okay, I'll take this one," I said and handed her the navy blue delicacy.

I also bought the powdery lavender bra with raised stitching that snaked around the cup. And I couldn't resist the Marie-Antoinette buttercream padded demi-cup style.

I had never paid so much for one bra and now I had purchased three Princesse Tam Tams.

I put my tired American relic into the crisp gold-and-white striped Princesse Tam Tam paper bag.

Should I hold onto the comfortable bra, or should I make a clean break with the past me, the plain, faded, earth-toned woman?

When I left the shop, I removed the sad, limp American bra that nestled in with the other beauties, and placed it in a wastebin. I carried my Princesse Tam Tam bag in lifted ecstasy. I hadn't been this gleeful for weeks.

I looked at my watch. My heart sank - the last bus back to Saint Mathieu de Tréviers left in 15 minutes.

I had just enough time to buy a rum raisin ice cream cone from the Häagen Dazs ice cream stand near the bus depot. I loved its creamy density mixed with cool rum, the raisins cold but chewy. Montpellier had stimulated my desire to have a life as delicious and decadent as the ice cream, a life filled with beautiful French lingerie. But I had to return to the convent where Lent was in full swing. Rum raisin was my consolation prize; there'd be none of this at the convent. I wanted to ingest more so that I would stay stuffed longer.

As I walked along the row of buses leaving Montpellier, I pushed the end of the pointed cone into my mouth, biting into the crunchy cookie and cold cream and was hit with a surge of sugary heaven. I climbed the steps into the bus: Number 23 to Saint Mathieu de Tréviers. Back to my home.

CHAPTER 12

ON CONVENT TIME

Bread, butter and jam for breakfast. Overcooked vegetables and a meat for lunch with more bread, wine and butter lettuce doused with a Dijon vinaigrette.

The meat was gristly and chewy without flavor or scent. The chef accused American cuisine of drowning everything in sauces, like the special sauce on a Big Mac. But almost every meat was drowned in sauce at Les Tourelles during the month I was there; how could he make that accusation? I didn't point out the inconsistency.

Very soon after the main course, we passed the cheese plate of Brie, Roquefort or another blue, and a semi-hard gouda-type. These cheeses were often the highlight of the meal for me. I loved the smooth texture of the Brie and its soft taste. The Roquefort, or maybe a close relative, was strong enough to lend some strength to the bland meal.

Immediately following the cheese, we passed a basket of oranges, apples and sometimes bananas and kiwis. The order and timing of these passings, which I was sometimes assigned to coordinate, caused anxiety for Agnes and Irene. When I did forget to fetch the fruit baskets from the kitchen, Agnes dramatically jumped up from the table. I suspected that forgetting the fruit basket could cause some calamity of European culinary culture and practice that I couldn't comprehend as an American.

After every meal, we cleared the tables, scraped the thin white plates of food, and loaded them into the dishwasher. Though the water in the machine was scalding hot, when the cycle ended, I would find pieces of food or grease on the wet steaming plates.

I didn't wear thong underwear at the convent. I wore an old pair of black leggings that would stretch too big after half an hour in them. A dark brown satin shirt covered my butt. I felt fat, unshapely, like the convent food. I watched the slow, heavy calories collect in my thighs and hips and arms and stomach - I couldn't get them moving, even though I walked up the hill behind the convent almost every day.

Some days I didn't cover my butt and would feel sorry for the aesthetic it presented in the dining room. Some days I wore a pair of dark blue cotton drawstring pants with white flecks that felt and looked like pajamas but were sold as karate pants at the GAP in Paris. I felt like a dumpling but there was no mirror to verify this.

I tried to figure out how to cure my constipation. Was it caused by the calcium-rich water or the wine I drank at both lunch and dinner? I craved crunchy salads of spinach, arugula, carrots, raw fennel and endive - and bread with the whole grain intact. I supplemented my leaden convent diet with Suchard Rocher Noir chocolate bon bons, dark chocolate candy bars, and boxes of crisp LU butter cookies. The onslaught of three meals a day, at regularly scheduled hours, disengaged my appetite sensors. I was never hungry. I was never full.

I didn't come to the convent to fill myself up but to empty myself out onto the page. I wrote to find clarity and direction. I didn't want to be fed any more distraction or stimulation, but the convent wasn't giving me what I craved. The afternoons during which I wrote were flat: it was still and hot outside, and light clouds obscured the sunlight. It was too quiet as I sat on my little bed with my laptop – where was everyone? Only the insects spoke. My legs hurt – I wanted to run, tire myself out, end the day exhausted. Instead, I stuck to the schedule: three meals a day, clean in the morning, write in the afternoon. And I had established this routine by day three.

Now I wanted to escape from the convent, like I had wanted to escape from Santa Barbara. At the convent, I thought I'd find a home, a spiritual respite, and be able to conquer my restlessness. I went to the French convent to find peace, meaning, and balance. The convent wasn't giving me peace; I wasn't finding any answers.

CHAPTER 13

JEROME

I stepped out of the shower, scrubbed clean of the chemicals that had splashed on me while I cleaned the men's toilets at the convent's conference center this morning. I could still smell the perfumed bleach in my nostrils. I wound the towel around my wet head and saw a Fed Ex letter laying on the floor of my room. It was from the U.S., from Jerome. My roommate in Paris must have forwarded the package to me at the convent.

Jerome's Fed Ex package contained a thick, left-justified letter with several subsections. "Will you be in Paris in June?" he wrote. I read the black text, sitting cross-legged on my narrow convent bed in rural France, thousands of miles from Jerome's condo in Alexandria, Virginia.

He also included a copy of a book review he wrote. On a yellow-lined Post-it note, he wrote that the review would explain how he has resolved his relationship with his ex-wife. I removed the Post-it and read his review of the book's stories on sailing and relationships: calm waters return after storms that had left tattered sails.

I had met Jerome ten years ago; we were crew members on a sailboat we raced on Lake Pepin, south of Saint Paul, before I moved to Santa Barbara. I picked up Jerome's letter and continued reading. On page five, he recalled an evening we spent drinking beers at Cognac McCarthy's in Saint Paul, soon after his wife had left him. Jerome told me that he was most attracted to me after I had swum my laps at the municipal pool, arriving at the bar with no makeup and short damp hair. "It's clear that my attraction to you was not a reaction to losing my wife but to something I'd found in you," he wrote.

"Before venturing onward, I must be candid," he warned me on the first page. He outlined his grand plan: a large house on many acres, transformed into a home, with his wife becoming a mother, and many dogs and kids running loose. The last gal didn't work out, he wrote. She didn't want children.

"I think there's a basis on which we could build a very good relationship," the letter ended.

I felt annoyed by his pronouncement of interest in exploring a possible relationship with me; it read like a legal brief. But he was it – the only attention I was getting from a man.

I looked out the large screenless window in my convent room that opened to the north. My room's one window faced a tangled assortment of trees and a meadow of charred vines. I looked out to an infinite North; clean, fresh, forward movement. The South felt stagnant, while East and West met each other to form an inescapably exhausting circle. The Herault wind blew loud like a passing semi-truck and then quieted to a low white noise, allowing the steady buzz of cicadas to grow louder. The scent of dry sage brightened the air.

I fantasized about circling the roundabout near the convent, heading north to the medieval town of Saint Guilhem, sitting in the leather passenger seat of a big black Mercedes, jeweled, and dressed in the blue tweed suit I had coveted in the Jaguar dress shop window on Rue du Faubourg Saint-Honoré in Paris. The warm scent of my expensive French perfume, Jean Patou's Sublime, a present from my Paris roommate, would complement the musky soft leather of the car's interior.

I wanted him to take me away, make it easy, be the right one, and relieve me of the work to make the wrong man the right one. I wanted what his money could provide: to make me feel special.

I wanted more than what Jerome offered. I wanted rich men with ranches. Rich men to take me out to fabulous restaurants. Rich men with houses in the Bahamas or the Virgin Islands. I wanted the Thomas Crowne Affair.

Living the life of a nun, leaving these desires unfulfilled, desires that tumbled constantly in my mind, would be impossible to endure for a lifetime.

But a love affair with Jerome, or Eric, or any man, broke a connection I had with myself, like a string snapping inside the case of a piano. The break happened almost unconsciously; it felt like I'd lost something but didn't know what it was. I became preoccupied with the state of repair of my lingerie or toenails. He pulled me like a magnet, attaching me to him, his interests, his moods or lack of them. I kept looking for that man who could fill me up. I was always sure it would work out.

One overcast afternoon in Paris, I walked into a cavernous church where I found a small altar to Saint Jude, the patron saint of hopeless causes. I lit a candle at the altar, wanting to believe that he was out there; we just kept missing each other.

The late afternoon Languedocian sun cast black shadows on the window glass. The bell rang for the 6:30 P.M. Vespers service. Dinner in an hour.

I put Jerome's thick pages back in the brown envelope. My mind flashed on a black and white photo I took of another man, a long time ago, lying back with his hands behind his head, round eyes looking straight into my camera lens. My head hurt. I didn't want to think about what I should have done – or could have done. Maybe I made some mistakes.

I made a lot of mistakes.

My mother visited me once in Santa Barbara. Compared to Minneapolis, Santa Barbara had very few libraries per capita, she informed me. She had arrived the day after I was dumped by a French academic whose farewell speech included "I know I could never love you - even if you had the perfect body."

That evening, I took my mother to Super Rica, Julia Child's favorite Mexican restaurant in Santa Barbara, famous for its small handmade corn tortillas filled with pork or pasilla chiles.

I sort of blamed my mother for my stupid behavior. I adopted her worldly interests and not-so-lightly veiled respect for power and wealth, and her belief that men were in charge. She talked a different story about the patriarchy but her actions didn't sync. I was easily seduced by sex and believed it would lead to some sort of perfect future with my sexual partner. Her particular brand of Catholicism branded me as a whore even though I hoped my promiscuity would yield true love. At Super Rica, I decided to share what she had wrought.

We sat on the tacqueria's cold open-air cement patio with inadequate space heaters and drank cans of Tecate. I heaped salsa on my pork taco while I recounted many of the lovers I'd had, summing up their fatal flaw in one sentence. Mike was too dependent on me. I couldn't deal with Hank's depression. My first boyfriend hit me. Then he raped me. (I didn't tell her that.) I worked hard to break Joe, the pious Catholic law student, and finally succeeded. And I also had sex with his roommate, a smart and sassy farm boy from Iowa who wore faded farmer jeans.

Then there was the Yugoslavian diplomat (married) and the young Saudi taking firefighter classes.

It was a confession.

But my sexual behavior was about the seduction of power too. As a student in Washington, D.C. during the end of the Carter Administration, my dorm mate and I hung out frequently at The Sign of the Dove on K Street. I could taste the power in that dark bar. Men wore gray suits and one night I met someone's body guard who told me that his gray-haired and trim client across the room was high up at the CIA. I flew to New York City to meet an Israeli arms dealer who took me to an Israeli Embassy party at a swanky hotel.

That behavior felt like ancient history, like my adolescent history with the Church. It was time to let the history go. I was at this convent with the invitation to Reprendre Souffle: to take time to breath. There were no men here and no one telling me what a bad Catholic I was. I was here with only myself to deal with.

Part of my desire to cloister myself at the convent was to think about all those men, what I had done wrong and what to do next. I wanted to be in a relationship. I thought I was choosing men more wisely. But I rarely chose: they chose me.

Men made me nervous, put me on stage, and forced me to perform. Like Jerome. He had a plan for me: his wife, our house, the kids, the dogs. But I knew he wasn't the one.

In the convent, I didn't have to watch myself, explain my behavior, or make excuses. Here, I got left alone. But I didn't want to be alone.

CHAPTER 14

SISTER ROSE

"Elizabeth, what do you cook at home for yourself in America?" Sister Rose asked me with a smile. We sat across from each other in the middle of the long dining room table, surrounded by mildly interested female eaters, mostly elderly, and the bright noon sun. Sister Rose's hair was short and light brown like mine and her face plain and sweet, no drama, no interest. Somebody said we resembled each other. Did I look that tired?

I struggled to recall any meal I had ever prepared in my narrow and bright yellow kitchen back in Santa Barbara. "Um, spinach salad with arugula, lots of salads, carrots," I replied, reflexively listing fresh produce we didn't get served at the convent. I looked down at the thick ham slice with a tiny bit of Dijon mustard on the edges and sauerkraut with peeled steamed potatoes in front of me: today's lunch in the convent dining room.

What I craved wasn't served at the convent: bread that contained the whole grain, crunchy raw vegetables. No wonder I was constipated.

She smiled, chewing politely, her fork resting easily in her hand. I asked Sister Rose, my look-alike, what she did for work. Three meals a day in the dining room, eating communally, facing someone familiar or strange across the long dining table, trying to find something interesting to say, exhausted me. But I felt I should play the hostess, a practice learned from my mom, who scolded me for being shy. The last time she noted this fault, I was 33 and we were sitting in the car about to meet the family of my brother's future wife. I admitted to her that I felt a little anxious and hoped they'd serve wine. "What a ridiculous thing to say!" she scolded. "Why on earth would you be nervous?"

I noticed Irene at the end of the table wasn't making any effort to be conversational. She leaned on one elbow while she ate the ham and potatoes. Her long blonde hair fell into the Dijon sauce on her plate as she looked absently out the window toward Saint Loup Peak.

Sister Rose worked as a nurse in Lyon and was here at the convent for her Easter vacation. Odd choice for a vacation, I thought, though nuns probably didn't go to Club Med or topless beaches at Spring Break – or any break.

I couldn't conjure up any more polite conversation and felt myself getting warm. The ham was tough and each bite required infinite chewing. The table was too quiet, all listening to the American.

I wanted to ask Sister Rose other questions, probing questions, but I worried that my questions were too intrusive. I wanted to understand when she decided to become a nun, but even more, I wanted to ask her what it was like to give up sex - forever.

She looked normal. She wore a sweater and jeans. She was tall and thin. I figured she wasn't raised any more religiously than I was. It would be hard to surpass my religious upbringing. But those shared variables didn't yield the same outcome: She made a radical decision. I felt I had rarely made a decision, only taken the next opportunity that put itself in front of me. Going to college, going to graduate school, getting a job. Those decisions were not radical.

The nuns at this convent had made a radical decision. But because I saw them frequently, they seemed as common as little robins. For some of them, maybe entering the nunnery was not a radical decision; perhaps other choices weren't available. Maybe Sister Jeanne wanted to marry but never found a suitable partner. She saw how some married women fare with their choice and decided that the coupled lifestyle was not what she wanted. Fall in love, marry, get pregnant and work the rest of your life cleaning, cooking and raising children – and serving a man.

These nuns chose a life with its rules too: they lived in community and as contemplatives; prayer was essential to their existence. They attended four services a day, starting with Laudes, at eight in the morning, and ending with Compline at eight-thirty at night, the only service I attended during my month sabbatical at the convent. It didn't seem their schedule allowed them much freedom to choose how to follow Jesus. Perhaps you needed rules to keep it going?

As a young girl, I used to believe that the nun route was all romanticism, fairy castle cathedrals and Gregorian chant and incense. Even later, I was pulled toward the mysticism of Hildegard de Bingem, Joan of Arc, Saint Thérèse of Lisieux. When I walked through musty cathedrals, awed by the light from colored window panes exposing fine dust particles hanging still in the air, the air cold and humid, I imagined these women living beautiful interior lives, reflected in the beautiful aesthetic of the cathedral's thrillingly dramatic architecture, gothic spires and gargoyles, and naves that rose several stories from the stone floor. Each sang Gregorian chant with her sisters from behind the altar, the musical tones tumbling over each other until their voices reached the rose window at the back of the cathedral.

Being chosen by God, choosing to put your inner life ahead of anything else: a job, lover, exercise regimen, ambition, even friends. The choice was so radical that centuries ago, women were burned for making it.

But the reality was much more mundane than my fantasies. There was little drama here. Life was pretty quiet on top of this hill in Languedoc.

A family friend who did her time in a nunnery of the 1950s is rumored to have left the convent because she was worked so hard, on her knees, scrubbing floors in a voluminous habit. From the snippets of family stories I heard as a girl, I imagined that her hands bled and that the old nuns made her work 12 hours a day. No mops, only buckets and brushes.

But she wouldn't have scrubbed 16th century stone floors in the U.S. The convent she eventually left sat on top of a hill in Southern Minnesota, built in the mid-twentieth century with donations from prosperous farmers and Mayo Clinic doctors. Her choices were different back then. A woman entering the convent today might work outside, in the larger community, like Sister Rose did.

Hayley Mills was somewhat responsible for my fascination with nuns. Her 1966 film "The Trouble with Angels" hooked me. Hayley was different from the other girls at the Catholic boarding school. She wasn't just a troublemaker, she was an individual, and she was not the nun type. The Mother Superior seemed icy until Hayley spied her crying from a church pew, bent over her nun friend's casket and sobbing.

I wanted more than a conventional life of marriage and children like the life for which Hayley's convent school friend Rachel was destined. At 10 years old, I was intrigued by Hayley's search for something more or different.

The nuns at the convent of Dominicaines des Tourelles lived in a cloister, separated from the rest of the world. But they left the cloister to welcome guests who came here for a retreat, which was part of their spiritual practice. They proselytized the Catholic theology to those who came for a guided retreat or to Sunday Mass, like their leader Saint Dominic did in the thirteenth century. Dominic likely had some connection with the Inquisition which had its main office in Languedoc. But these nuns did not burn heretics at the stake. Instead, they hosted conferences with Jesuit scholars.

I was surprised to see Sister Rose on the hiking trail behind the convent buildings. Almost every day at 5:00 P.M., I would put on my running shoes while the sun was still high in mid-April and two hours remained before the dinner bell rang.

The limestone trail was wide enough for a truck and bordered by lavender and little yellow and white flowers. I knew I was halfway to the top of the hill when I passed a crumbling stone shack that looked several centuries old.

Though I loved the beauty of the dry rocky terrain, the fragrant pines and spindly deciduous trees along the path, I was intent on getting to the top and down with speed. I wanted to burn some calories before I ate and drank more of them at dinner.

I also wanted the high that climbing the hill gave me so I pushed myself. It was both penance and pleasure. I felt strong, red-blooded. It cleared my mind of thoughts about how tired I was of the routine of cleaning convent rooms every day and the faint scent of chlorine in the sliced baguette we ate for breakfast every morning.

I saw Sister Rose coming down the trail as I was going up. "Bonjour, Elizabeth!" she called out to me. I slowed down, smiling, giving her the opportunity to start a conversation. But she never took it. Sister Rose didn't look pressed for time, just out for a late afternoon stroll. She was happy without knowing who I was. She smiled at me and kept walking.

After dinner, Agnes and I leaned against the large sink in the dishwashing room while we waited for the dishwasher to do its job. The square white robot chugged and steamed and then spit out the pile of dirty dinner dishes that we had stacked earlier and sent through its large mouth.

"You are so lucky," Agnes said as we grabbed the hot dishes as they emerged from the steaming commercial dishwasher. "You can be single in the West and not feel the pressure to marry. I'm old at 27; I should be married by now." Agnes grew up in a small town in the Czech Republic, the daughter of two classical musicians. She worked as a nurse in Prague before coming to the convent several months ago to perfect her French. Agnes's plight reminded me of my Parisian roommate's despair at being single at 34.

I didn't feel as free as Agnes assumed. I also felt the cultural strictures that strongly encouraged marriage and reproduction for women. I suspected some considered me an oddity at 42: neither nun nor mother. I didn't even have a divorce to explain my spinster situation. I hadn't achieved great things professionally. So what had I done with my time?

I didn't have a baby in which to bundle my creativity. I hadn't settled on the One Man who theoretically could satisfy the many desires a woman is supposed to have: building a nest, creating a life together.

Sister Rose got the calling to serve Jesus. She didn't get the calling to have sex – lucky girl? I wanted to ask her about this but didn't have the right words. I was afraid I'd insult her with my assumptions.

But she and I did share one spiritual calling: the love of hiking a trail.

CHAPTER 15

SECRETS

I stayed up late one night until after one in the morning, drinking the local red Faugères wine I had bought at the Intermarché supermarket in town. I drank three small glasses. The convent's wine glasses were short and round, with no stem: un verre. Everything was drunk out of these sturdy glasses. After lunch each day, I would pour coffee for a guest into the glass when a bit of wine still colored its bottom.

The recycling bin next to the handyman's tool room was always full of liquor bottles – wine bottles and other types too. I couldn't imagine any of the nuns drinking hard liquor and the typical guest at the convent was also a nun or related to one of the nuns or a hunched-over old woman. The empty bottles were black or red with odd long shapes that hinted at cheap liqueurs, not fine Armagnacs. I wondered how much I wasn't seeing.

The nuns' living quarters were separate from the areas the rest of us inhabited. We au pairs didn't clean the rooms in their cloister. Any information about the nuns came from my co-workers who had been at the convent for several months, but the news was sparse. I picked up some information about their habits but never got enough to satisfy my curiosity.

At Passion Sunday lunch, I set the tables for 50 people with old china in two different faded floral patterns. I had watched the nuns' excitement at opening the doors of the cupboards near the kitchen. Inside, the shelves were stocked with the chipped Limoges plates and I wondered if this special china was part of a dowry for an expected marriage but instead had followed one of these women to the convent.

I also wondered about the priest who lived at the convent. He ate lunch alone at a square table, feeding soup into his old unevenly shaven mouth, wearing huge black-rimmed square glasses and a white scarf around his neck, a la Yves Saint Laurent. The scarf fell over his cheap-looking camelhair jacket which he wore no matter what the temperature. I asked Sister Jeanne why the priest ate alone at a separate table, away from the au pairs but not with the nuns in their cloister. Her explanation confused me. "He lives with us," she explained, "but he is very discreet. He doesn't hear the nuns' confessions - they bring in a different priest for that." I wondered if the loaner priest ever heard confessions of unrequited love.

I suspected that this priest ate alone to escape having to endure poorly spoken French by me and my fellow au pairs and the small talk of elderly women at every meal.

Irene and another au pair surreptitiously made a chocolate cake one evening. Since it was Lent, eating sweets was forbidden at the convent until Easter Sunday. The two

Norwegians had to enlist the aid of Jean-Pierre the Chef to complete the sinful task. Did the nuns detect the smell of the warm chocolate slithering uninhibitedly from the ovens and through their cloister walls? Had I chosen to stay at the convent during a non-Lenten month, would the food be better? Would we get dessert after dinner?

I noticed that Sister Josephine, the Mother Superior, was served red meat at every meal, even during Lent, for some condition which remained a mystery. Of all the nuns, she was in the best shape. Sister Clare was obese; perhaps she ate in secret? When the nuns completed the last of the four offices at 9:00 P.M., the Compline service, did they then separately retire to their rooms with a glass of cognac? Or maybe they got together and got drunk occasionally?

My coworkers didn't drink; I had to. I justified my consumption as an opportunity to drink local and interesting wines that would be difficult or impossible to find back home. My inebriation wasn't an escape but a method of reinhabiting myself after a day of playing someone I didn't know.

I spoke French all day. They called me Elizabeth, a play name. My grandmother had called me Elizabeth in her Slovak accent; now I heard it in a French one. All morning I wore a blue apron, identifying me as a maid. I carried buckets and cleaning chemicals. I respected the hierarchy of rags when I used three different types to clean a guest room. I always verified this order with a coworker before starting my chore. I showed up on time for breakfast, lunch and dinner, hungry or not.

At the lunch table, I poured myself a glass of red table wine. I wanted to drink the whole bottle. I was in a coma induced by heavy food and cleaning chemicals. I tried to find time to take a shower before lunch but usually had to sit at the table and eat, knowing that my pants were sprayed with chemicals and that a film of dust covered my hair and skin.

To live here all your life: Sister Bernadette for 27 years, Sister Clare for 20. To eat together three times a day and then pray together four times a day. No wonder Sister Clare was fat. Love for Jesus doesn't keep the demons away. Of course there were secrets. Strange behaviors too. The rigidity surrounding time was obsessive. There were so many obligations each day, every day was the same.

Maybe the convent was full of depressed women who needed a schedule to keep their chemically imbalanced brains on track. Perhaps children, a husband – too much of a mess to manage. But life with Jesus seemed kind of hard too.

Maybe the order was why they drank. Order requires disorder to achieve balance. They belonged to the Dominican Order of nuns. The pope/bishop/priest/male authority ordered them to do this and not that. Of course they drank.

But order was good for a person. This belief had me sign up for a French class during my two months in Paris to give my free-form days some necessary structure. I felt like I was treading water and hoped I'd feel more mentally stable if I erected a swimming lane for at least two hours a day. Work, workout, and maintain a healthy level of social interaction. Don't eat too much sugar or again, the chemical imbalance that you are stuck with, damned to hell with, will act up and tip that sanity scale.

But madness would have been preferable to the lackluster sameness of days. Maybe this was why I drank. I needed a break from this sameness.

What did it matter? My emotional imbalance made me so sad already – what was a little alcohol going to hurt? It made the hurt worse. Alcohol was a viper. It bit and left worse than any sting: It left despair and an upset tummy.

CHAPTER 16

SISTER JOSEPHINE'S CHOIR

Sister Josephine left her sitar and walked around the table to point to the whole note on the sheet of music flat on the table in front of me. She stood over me and loudly scolded about the difference between whole notes and half notes. She thought I didn't know how to count them. I wanted to tell her the difference so she would know that I knew the difference, but I didn't know French music vocabulary.

Sister Josephine pissed me off.

Sister Josephine was the Prioress, the Head Nun, Mother Superior. I wasn't afraid of her scolding. I wasn't interested in knowing her either. I didn't think she'd have the patience to get to know me - my French wasn't good enough.

I suspected that Sister Josephine came from a wealthy family. She had a hauteur, an air of having been well educated. She was slender, tall, dark blonde hair, very efficient in her white pullover and white cotton skirt.

We choristers sat in a bright white conference room at a long table, me next to Agnes, my Czech co-worker. Sister Josephine and Sister Patrice were co-directing the choir for the upcoming services of Holy Week. Today was our second rehearsal. I was here because Sister Jeanne invited some of us au pair girls to sing with the nuns.

Sister Patrice directed us while Sister Josephine stood next to her at the sitar, overruling her direction. I didn't understand the words but Sister Josephine's handsome face was set rigidly and she ignored Sister Patrice, who sighed. "I'm amazed that the nuns let us see them bicker like this," Agnes whispered to me. The other nuns at the table sat quietly, their faces flat.

My fellow worker Irene had earlier told me that Sister Patrice, the former Mother Superior, wore a wig because she lost all her hair from breast cancer 40 years ago. Her hair and the cancer never came back. I wondered if Sister Josephine colored her hair that had no gray.

Sister Jeanne and Sister Bernadette, the young nuns, were slated to be the soloists at the Easter services. Sister Bernadette did the accounting for the Dominicaines des Tourelles convent. I sat behind Bernadette who wore jeans and a wool pullover, the convent uniform. She looked about 40, like a sailor, very sporty. Short dull brown hair, a chinless profile. Her singing voice surprised me: soft and high, in contrast to her butch style.

Sister Jeanne's voice was soft and high too, like Bernadette's. Jeanne came from Alsace and looked like the Dutch girl on a chocolate tin. Yesterday, I was surprised to hear her girlie laugh from the convent kitchen as I hung a wet towel on a rack in the dish room. Her sergeant style dominated her role as manager of the convent's guesthouse, and as au pair boss. Agnes whispered to me that Sister Josephine yelled at her.

I caught Sister Clémence looking at me and she looked away. I knew she thought I was strange, working as a maid at my age. The other au pairs were young, in college. And I was from America, where everyone is rich. Didn't I have enough money to take a proper vacation and pay for it?

I didn't know anyone normal that would do this: work at a convent for a month for free room and board. Other people would take their two-week vacation and pay for a nice hotel.

But in a hotel, I wouldn't get to sing. And I was drawn to this world, otherwise, why would I choose to spend a month here? I admitted that I had always been curious about nuns but it was more than that. These women had intimate relationships with each other – they lived communally, connecting on a spiritual level, married to the same being: Jesus. They belonged to something bigger than their individual selves.

Me, I was like the sun: everything revolved around me. I got anxious when my needs weren't met, especially those I demanded from a lover. This month at the convent was a detox camp; I was taking a break from tripping from one man to another. And despite Sister Josephine, for the month of April that I lived and worked at the convent, I got to sing psalms with French nuns, getting ready for Easter, for the Resurrection.

Every evening after dinner, we au pairs washed, dried and put the dinner dishes into the large cupboards next to the dining room. We then set the breakfast bowls and dishes on the just-wiped tables after counting how many guests Sister Jeanne expected for breakfast the next morning. My duties done, I left the dining room, walked down the hallway and into the small round chapel for the Compline service.

The Compline service was the final of the four offices performed every day at the convent. The nuns' day started with Laudes (Morning Prayer) at 8:00 A.M., Mass at 11:30 A.M., just before lunch, then Vespers (Evening Prayer) at 6:15 P.M., just before dinner, and finally Compline (Night Prayer) at the end of the day. On Thursday, the "jour de desert" or the desert day, the nuns hid away all day in their cloister and no offices took place.

The Compline service ended work for the day and released me to the evening. Sitting in the dark chapel erased my irritation at again forgetting and again having to be reminded to turn on the dishwasher before dinner so that the water would be hot and the robot would be ready to load with dirty dishes as soon as we finished eating, my disappointment in the quality of the uneven local wine at dinner, my anger at the little time I got to myself and the large amount of time I spent setting and clearing tables. My reward: I got to sing throughout the entire Compline service, except where Sisters Jeanne or Bernadette had small solos. Psalm 93, in French - the same each night.

The Compline service's only activity was chanting the Psalms. No sermon, no priest, just singing for thirty minutes in the candle-lit small round chapel.

We sat against the rounded wall on wooden benches that held the outer perimeter of the chapel: fifteen nuns on the left wall, and a few convent guests and me on the right. I took a breath, and sound came out. Voices moved around me, singing the same note but with different colors. They filled the round sparsely-decorated chapel, quickly bounced off the white plaster walls, and filled the empty spaces between us.

To signal the end of the service, Sister Clémence left the nuns' side of the round chapel to turn off the only light. In the near-dark, I could smell the warm beeswax candles. Sister Clémence then blew out two candles, leaving the candle under the Virgin Mary icon lit.

I looked across the chapel at the nuns who sat here every night, like a family. Their faces were expressionless. Maybe they were tired. Then one left, then another.

One night, I sat until everyone left, even the last nun who blew out the candle under the Virgin Mary icon. My body still hummed from the vibration created by the voices chanting the last Psalm. I was wide awake, gleeful, sitting alone in the dark. My legs felt solid, my back straight against the wall, perfectly balanced.

Ten years ago, I sang this Compline service with a small Gregorian chant choir at Saint Mark's Church in Minneapolis one Sunday evening a month. Our voices mixed with the candlelight and incense that rose up into the gothic spheres of the ceiling. I never thought about what the service meant; I just liked to sing it, enunciate the Latin vowels, and sustain the high soprano notes. I felt small, like a sparkly jewel, singing in that still architecture, in the dark.

In the convent chapel, I wasn't performing like I did in Minneapolis; I was singing to myself. Or maybe I was singing with this community. And I didn't have to leave at the end of the service and drive home. I was home.

CHAPTER 17

AGNES'S MUSIC

I sat on my little twin bed with Agnes's Walkman in my ears, listening to Ida Kelarová. She sang a chant with another voice accompanying her, a piano played alone, one note at a time, then a male voice entered. The piano rushed in with a simple flowing melody.

Agnes told me that Ida Kelarová was from Moravia, a region of the Czech Republic. The word Moravian conjured up gypsies, mystery, and dark-haired magic. She told me that Ida used Moravian folk songs and improvised with modern jazz techniques, but this was not jazz that I'd ever heard.

Another chant. I imagined Arabia, North Africa. A woman cried passionately. A choir of women joined her. The words were Gypsy, or Czech? Something Slavic, the underwater sound of the language.

Agnes didn't respond to American music like Irene and the other au pairs did. I wondered if Agnes purposely avoided American music and instead championed the music of the Moravians and Gypsies - groups that didn't have a contract with Warner Bros.

She stayed apart from the others, this nonwestern European. She told me that I was the only one that knew where her country was because I had visited her hometown of Litomyšl just two years ago when my brother and I took my father to his parent's village in Slovakia. We are countrywomen, I felt her declare. She invited me to the folk concerts in Slovakia and the Czech Republic that took place in the summer in the mountains. I felt as though I filled her emptiness, like a fairy godmother.

Agnes adored Rimbaud. Her cell was crowded with his poetry and other used hardback poetry books she had purchased in Montpellier. Along the wall, cards made from the brown thin paper unique to France, hung on a string and clipped with clothespins. She had written French verse on some and English on others. She spoke so fast and excitedly while she gave me a tour of her room and its literary contents that spit gathered between her white teeth.

She had lived at the convent for several months, longer than any of the other au pairs. She wanted to work with a French medical team in Africa and needed to speak French well. The convent provided French lessons but brought out her darkness. She brooded.

Agnes was passionate - something I suspected I lacked. What was my passion? I had never strung up poems. Though I did love music, I had never invested in a sound system. I listened to music from my Toyota Tercel's cassette player or from the boom box a friend gave me for sitting her house and dog for a week in Ojai.

Several nights during my month at the convent, Irene from Norway, Maryam from Germany, Agnes, sometimes

Stephan, and I, would gather in the lounge. We sat on the floor around the low coffee table and on the large soft sofa. We drank tea and sang Beatles songs. These young women, except for Maryam, knew the lyrics and the guitar chords. Irene played her mandolin. Agnes had a recorder and drums. I had only my voice and a rudimentary familiarity with the lyrics of Yesterday and Hey Jude from playing them on the piano when I was younger. I was impressed that these young women were so talented, could sing well and play instruments. They all seemed to have a natural talent for music.

Agnes offered to teach me Moravian folk songs one night but didn't show up in the common room when we had agreed to meet. I found her later with Renée, a frequent convent guest from Italy, playing the recorder. She had changed her plans without telling me. I consoled myself with a stereotype: Czechs were not to be trusted - their word was as good as air - just like my Slovak grandmother said.

During Holy Week, Agnes asked me to trim her hair. She just wanted the back trimmed. Still, I was nervous. I hadn't cut hair since high school when I would trim the hair on my mother's neck so that the top layers of her hair would curve under in a bob.

I entered her room, her poetry cell, crammed with books, on chairs, on the floor. She immediately offered to lend me her black dress for Easter. It was sleeveless and form-fitting. I was able to put it on over my head and keep my pants on until I had to pull the dress over my butt. Too tight. I tried to hide my fraying underpants while I pulled it up and off my body.

"How short do you want me to cut it?" I asked. I didn't know Agnes very well. How vain was she? What kind of cutting mistake would she tolerate?

"I want it to be shorter in the back," she responded, grabbing the black shafts of hair on her neck. Just like my mom wanted.

"OK," I said, holding my breath. I had to plunge in. Her hair was difficult because it was thick and stick-straight, straighter than mine. An uneven cut would be noticed. Her hair was already pretty short.

I picked up the scissors she had taken from the linen room. She pulled her faded gray t-shirt off over her head. Underneath she wore what used to be a white bra. The thin dingy fabric was held together by several large safety pins. I was stunned.

I wondered if she had seen my new navy Princesse Tam Tam bra when I tried on her too-tight black dress.

"Wow – your bra is a work of art! So many pins!" But I didn't say that – I was too embarrassed for her – and ashamed. I was a rich woman compared to Agnes. My retirement account would support me for six months, as long as I kept my Princesse Tam Tam fetish under control.

"OK, put your head down," I directed, and started cutting.

"How do you afford to live in France for so many months?" I asked her.

"I'm lucky," she explained. "I used to work for a German man whose wife was dying and he sends me money once in a while. Yesterday, he sent me 200 marks; that's a lot of money." As I cut her hair, in the middle of her little room,

I realized that I didn't know anything about her life. She didn't have any photos for me to guess about. Irene had two photos of a boy standing next to her, both of them wearing prom-type clothing. But I didn't ask her about them. There were so many other things to talk about. The absence of men at the convent had us forget about their existence.

"Why did you come to France?" she asked.

"I planned to come two years ago because I love the language and the culture and just wanted to live in it for a while but I met a man and fell in love. After we broke up, I decided it was time." This was not the whole story but it was true.

I wondered if this information cleared anything up for Agnes. Did she think I was a lesbian? I was older, single, staying in a convent. Never married, no children. What did she think of the weekly phone call from my parents in Minneapolis? Old maid, attached to her parents? Once I got to the convent, they began calling me during dinner. A nun would find me in the dining room and I'd leave the table, walk out of the dining room, down the hallway past the conference room, and into the small box that contained the phone. It was usually my mother who called.

Agnes may have wanted more information but I didn't want to dredge up anything that happened before I got to the convent. My history seemed so heavy; better to just let it rest for now. I was here, in France, speaking a different language, being a different person almost. I didn't want to explain my past in the U.S. in French. I wanted to get away from it. I'd be back in the U.S. soon enough, speaking English to Americans about my month in the convent.

While I carefully snipped away small black pieces of her hair, I listened to her throw out French in a stream, heavily accented with Slavic vowels. She could speak several languages but she didn't have the music of French. She smiled when she spoke which made the vowels more difficult for me to comprehend. Still, she was fun to talk with.

I began to talk like she did: I threw out the words without first mentally verifying verb tense agreement. I took that risk. She was my countrywoman.

PART III

CHAPTER 18

SHOPPING AT THE GAP

When I arrived at the convent, at the start of April, a black field of charred stumps grew on one side of the dirt road leading from the convent into the town of Saint Mathieu de Tréviers. The stumps were thick and old. I knew they were grape vines but they looked dead, unlike the willowy vines that attached to trellises in the Santa Ynez Valley near Santa Barbara. I took a photo each week as the black gnarled stumps popped out tiny fresh buds that opened florescent green against the charred wood. When I left the convent in early May, hardy green leaves completely hid the old stumps.

My body changed too: it needed spring clothes. It was too warm to wear heavy black spandex leggings, a dark brown blouse or a gray wool sweater. I was forced to go shopping.

Irene met me in Montpellier on my second journey to the big city. She wore black and gray too. We wandered through the large Polygone shopping mall and entered a bookstore. She bought a French fashion encyclopedia and I bought a Michelin map of the Aquitaine, a region on the Atlantic coast. I planned on exploring that foie gras land when I left the convent.

A furniture store displayed clean-lined teak chairs and tables, colorful Marimekko-print linen fabrics, and contemporary-styled forks and spoons. Irene told me she loved these kinds of stores and couldn't wait to have a house filled with these treasures. I loved walking through furniture stores too but felt like an observer, never a potential buyer. I had a checkered history with furniture stores.

On Sundays after Mass, my dad would drop my sister and Mom and me off at Gabberts, the Twin Cities' premier furniture store. My mother would take us girls down to the basement, a fantasyland for children abandoned by mothers whose fantasy was furnishing the house with the furniture upstairs. The last time I was in Gabberts on one of my semiannual visits to Minneapolis, my sister and I listened to my mother tell stories while we drank hot chocolate. We sat at a glass-topped patio table with curly-cue yellow iron chairs next to the kid-sized water wheel whose lake shimmered with shiny pennies lying on the bottom. The hot chocolate machines had been replaced but the roar of the machines was familiar, except that I could regulate how much liquid I wanted in the styrofoam cup before letting go of the button to fill the rest of the cup with creamy brown foam.

As children, my sister and I sat in this lounge at small kid-sized wooden desks in front of a TV and watched *Gilligan's Island* while our mother roamed the showrooms upstairs. She left us alone, with all the other abandoned kids.

Gabberts had since moved the TV into the corner, up high and shining down like a searchlight. The room seemed more like a sports bar than a children's garden. A man in running attire sat alone like an unbalanced stalk growing from one of the small desks, watching a CNN report. I suspected his wife had deposited him here while she roamed the rooms upstairs. Two kids watching TV had an adult wedged into a little desk next to them. I noticed they weren't eating Animal Crackers.

I had already opened all the doors under the coffee, hot chocolate, and hot water machines, looking for the boxes of Animal Crackers. Nothing.

When I came back to the table with no Animal Crackers, my mother told me that she had been able to get them recently by telling one of the furniture salespeople that she had a migraine headache. She said they kept them in the filing drawers right outside the water wheel room, next to a desk where a saleswoman now stood. She and I left our purses and hot chocolate with my sister at the glass table to secure some Animal Crackers.

The saleswoman next to the drawers was completing a sale with a customer and waiting for the receipt to exit the printer. Should I tell her I have a migraine, my mother whispered to me? No, let's just ask for a couple of boxes, I said.

I really wanted the Animal Crackers and didn't care that I wasn't getting them for a child or what the saleswoman would think of me. The drawers have changed since I was here last, my mom noted.

I realized that I was responsible for securing the Animal Crackers; my mother hung back. I waited until the saleswoman had torn the receipt from the printer and handed it to the customer before I asked if she knew where I could get some Animal Crackers. She smiled and opened a drawer stuffed with the colorful animated boxes of Animal Crackers. She handed me three boxes.

Like little girls, we giggled back to our water wheel-side table, each with a box. They were crisp and fresh, perfect with the hot chocolate. I ate my box, my sister's and half of my mom's.

The Animal Crackers had withstood all the furniture style changes Gabberts had made through the decades: The modern black leather strap and chrome chairs of the 1970s and the chintz love seats of the 1980s were gone, replaced by overstuffed sofas covered in heavy red cotton that I would have liked for myself.

As I walked through this French furniture store with Irene, I thought of my mother looking at furniture for decades, hanging back. When she finally did buy some for the living room, I had already finished graduate school.

Next to the furniture store in the Polygone mall was a clothing store selling linen skirts and cropped blouses in soft pastel colors. I wanted to dress in these loose clothes and walk fluidly in the Mediterranean sun, like a dancer. The prices were outrageous.

French clothes were expensive if made from quality fabrics in linen or cotton. Most of the stores in the Polygone mall sold skirts and pants made of polyester. The texture of the fabric made me cringe. I couldn't wear these garments against my body even though they were inexpensive.

The GAP was on the third floor of the mall, the American solution to my problem. It would have quality cotton clothes at decent prices. But I was embarrassed that I wanted to shop at this hegemonic American store. I hoped Irene's opinion of me as a Europhile wouldn't crumble when she saw that I preferred some U.S. products to European ones.

The GAP was packed with young women. It looked like a GAP in any U.S. mall but here the clothes were crowded more closely together. We squeezed between customers and clothes racks to get to the pants rack. Everything was smaller in France, including the GAP.

The young saleswomen didn't greet us or offer to assist us. They probably knew I was American and despised that the GAP was my store, part of my national identity. I was in their country and should support the French culture by purchasing French garments. It was the Starbucks ethical dilemma. The GAP was taking over: it was affordable, it was good quality, it was fresh, and it was American. And I needed cotton and couldn't afford French cotton prices. Some days it reached 80 degrees at the convent and I couldn't breathe in my black spandex leggings.

Since I was without sales help, Irene offered to fetch pants for me while I waited in my underwear in the tiny dressing room. I hadn't seen my body in a mirror in almost three weeks. The mirror in my convent room was over the sink, large enough to see only my face and neck while I brushed my teeth. What size was I now? I felt bigger and wigglier. I was a size 6 at home but asked Irene to get me sizes 8, 10 and 12. I felt both relief and despair that the 8 fit.

I chose a neutral color – light, like the limestone the convent sat on. The price of the crisp cropped khaki pants was marked in both francs and dollars. These expensive pants, not on sale, would initiate my new wardrobe and serve as a base for more beauty in my life. This forward, positive thinking was sufficient rationalization for the hefty credit card purchase. Since I had already put five Princesse Tam Tams on the card, this purchase would only marginally increase my VISA bill balance. And I did not want to hang back like my mother had.

I got my hair cut too – short, cropped above my ears. Renée, the convent guest from Italy, told me that the beauty school in Montpellier gave haircuts as stylish as the celebrity salon in the tourist district did – for a quarter of the price.

The cutter's confidence silenced me as hair clumps began to rapidly cover the linoleum floor and the shape of my skull emerged. I hadn't been able to tell her what I wanted before she began cutting – I was too intimidated by what I figured was superior training to any she could have gotten in the U.S.

When the cutter gave me the mirror, pronouncing the job complete, my watch told me the last bus to the convent was about to depart.

Irene and I ran back to the bus depot with enough time to get ice cream cones at Häagen Dazs before boarding the Number 23 bus back to Saint Mathieu de Tréviers.

Sister Jeanne was the first to evaluate my metamorphosis – shorn on top and cropped at my ankles. This was the most skin that I'd revealed at the convent.

"Ah, très jolie!" she exclaimed when she saw me that evening at choir rehearsal for the Holy Week services. Did she mean I was now pretty or that I looked nice? Jolie – another ambiguous French word. I decided to go with pretty.

CHAPTER 19

HOLY THURSDAY

The Holy Thursday Mass celebrated the Last Supper and included a reenactment of Jesus washing the feet of his apostles. The convent invited the community of Saint Mathieu de Tréviers to the Mass and to the special supper following it. Sister Jeanne asked me if I would be one of the apostles. I couldn't believe it. I was The American! Why did they want an American, and a woman too, sitting up on the altar, as an apostle? There were plenty of nuns to fill the role. Did I have nicer feet to wash?

I sat on a folding chair in a line up with the other apostles on the altar. We had removed our shoes and socks. My feet were very white.

Families with young children and old couples packed the small round chapel at the Convent of Tourelles. I had never seen so many people in the chapel. Though the mood was reverent, the air buzzed.

The priest began the Jesus Washing the Feet of His Disciples ritual by kneeling next to a metal cake pan filled with water at the end of the apostle line up. I was number one. The act of having an old wiry priest in a cloth robe kneel in front of me and bend over my feet while he ran a wet washcloth over my two feet was confusing. It didn't feel sexual or holy. It was sweet. No one had ever washed my feet with such kindness and attention. I had earlier feared I might burst out laughing over this play-acting but the event was too solemn.

My role at the convent had changed since I'd arrived three weeks ago. I was not just a foreign maid who cleaned toilets and changed beds. I was now a member of the choir and would perform at all the Easter services during Holy Week. I was asked to be an apostle. Sister Jeanne even told me that I was a good addition to the au pair team, that my sense of humor lightened the dour mood of the younger girls. I was moved that she differentiated me from the pack of foreign guest workers.

I knew I was different – I was American, a rarity here, one of the first.

Sister Jeanne also told me that I was a good diplomat. I was surprised that she noticed that I didn't get defensive with all the stereotypical crap my dining partners threw at me, such as my assumed elevated opinion of McDonald's cuisine, or when they blamed me for Clinton's bad foreign policy moves.

I hadn't been to many Holy Week services since graduating from high school. When my fiancé and I vacationed in Santa Fe, it happened to be Lent and we wandered into the cathedral during Passion Sunday Mass. We stayed throughout the reading of the Passion, an unholy amount of time. I felt uncomfortable, an imposter, and wanted to leave. But Paul, my fiancé, a non-Catholic, seemed like he was enjoying it so I didn't say anything. After we broke up, Paul married a Catholic woman at the Santa Barbara Mission. Over lunch shortly after the event, he told me that when his wife got angry at him, she really lit into him. I hadn't done that in a long time. This was what I was missing in my single state in the convent: yelling at each other, forgiving each other, repeat.

I wanted to yell at that Jesuit. His lecture, only two weeks ago, seemed silly now. And my defensive reaction was silly too. Let him have his theology and his Rules and judgment. Whatever it got him, he didn't look like a very happy man.

That evening in the dishwashing room, Agnes told me in a lowered voice that she didn't like large groups of Catholics. I agreed, especially the ones that have The Family as their agenda. Earlier that week, we watched such a group called "Action Catholique sur la Famille" pull up to the convent's main building in a bus, 50 of them, mostly women. Their driver told us au pairs that he didn't want to eat with them. Could he please eat early? Irene told him he'd have to wait 15 minutes until lunch was ready but he didn't seem to understand. Then Stephan stepped in to clarify, the native French speaker on our au pair team.

"I'm embarrassed to tell you this," Agnes confessed to me, her fellow Catholic au pair, while we set the table for dinner. Six years ago, she was chosen among many young Prague Catholics to fly to Denver to attend Pope John Paul II's Mass. "I was very devout," she said. I told her that while I lived in Paris, I wandered in and out of beautiful churches, but I refused to stay for Mass. Just thinking about Mass made my body hair stand up like a cat's, backed up against the wall, only I was captive in a pew.

And Maryam. She went to Mass for the first time at the Holy Thursday service. She even went up to the altar to take Communion. I wondered what the nuns thought: a Turkish Muslim eating the body of Christ!

But tonight, they had asked me to participate, not to fill out a questionnaire. There was no test of my "faith." I didn't have to sacrifice myself to be a member of this community.

I didn't sacrifice myself to marry Paul either. We made an attractive couple and everybody loved him. I suspected some thought I was crazy not to marry him.

I called Paul the day before he married to tell him that I really appreciated the invitation to his wedding but I just couldn't face watching him get married. Of course he understood, he said. I was happy for him but I didn't want to watch the backs of two people in love making a vow for life. It wasn't about him, it was about feeling like a loser. I didn't follow the Rules. I didn't marry the suitable partner. Maybe there will never be one. I may always be alone. But I stayed true to myself. And I wasn't alone tonight, on Holy Thursday, the Last Supper, when Jesus and his friends ate dinner together. I was amazed that in one month, I too had a community who knew me and had invited me to join them.

CHAPTER 20

GOOD FRIDAY

On Good Friday, the most somber day of Holy Week, the day Jesus was nailed to a cross, and in the last week of my month-long sabbatical, a black woman with cornrows appeared at the dining room table for dinner. Her round ample body was wrapped in African yellow and green fabric. When Sister Jeanne gave us our work duty that morning after breakfast, she told us that a new guest had arrived from Ghana, or maybe Zambia. The contrast of this black woman at a table of bland white women focused all our attention on her. I wondered about the relationship between Africa and France, the history of colonialism and Catholicism and what her story was in that historical mix.

I sat across from her at the dinner table and listened to her talk about her life in Toulouse, a city southwest of the convent. But her accent wasn't African – no rolled Rs. She didn't speak like the Africans I had heard in Paris. Her accent sounded almost American. I asked this beautiful woman if she grew up in Toulouse.

"I'm from Los Angeles," she smiled. Los Angeles! I laughed and switched to English. She told me she met a French man when she danced with a troupe many years ago. She moved to Toulouse, married him and now had a teenaged daughter. We talked about Los Angeles, and the au pairs laughed when I called it L.A. It was so easy to speak, too easy. But I didn't like how my voice sounded, its lazy American vowels against the crisp French enunciation that required advanced mouth gymnastics to perfect. The flat lazy tones of our English sat back in their lounge chairs with a drink and a cigarette while the stiff, gilded Louis XIV chairs around us at the table fell silent, but stayed alert, listening.

This was too easy, speaking English with the African from L.A. And it was cheating too. I felt a polite interest from the old women at the other end of the table while she and I compared our Southern California lives. Oh, Elizabeth is speaking English. And then they fell back into the description of a glorious meal consumed years ago, while sawing at the flavorless and colorless meat on their plates.

Me alone, at the dinner table, at battle against a French ideal that lived undisturbed and unquestioned in each of these old French women's bodies and minds. Besides, I was a guest, not a conqueror. I was here to embrace the language, the culture, the country. Defending the U.S. felt exhausting; where to start?

At the table, Agnes suggested that we play music in the lounge and sing with our new American friend after dinner and cleaning up. Besides Agnes's guitar and Irene's mandolin, Agnes had drums and a recorder too.

Good Friday had the convent grounds in lock-down. Nothing was happening tonight – Christ had died and we were all waiting for him to rise on Sunday morning with a sneak preview at the Easter Vigil ceremony on Saturday night. The nuns were cloistered in their cloister, doing what nuns do on Good Friday, this darkest day in the Catholic liturgical calendar.

We five au pairs and our new American friend met in the lounge with instruments. We were all very excited but Agnes was ecstatic. She carried both her tom toms and a large drum. This woman had brought her to life – she had been resurrected early!

"Where can we dance?" our new African friend asked.

"In the chapel!" yelled Agnes. We all laughed and looked at each other, eyes wide. Dancing in the chapel! Would we get in trouble, asked Irene?

We carried the drums down the dark hallway of the main building, walking silently past the empty dining room and into the dark chapel. We danced around the altar while the Virgin Mary and Infant looked down at us from their perch where Sister Clémence lit and blew out the candle that illuminated the Russian Orthodox print each night at the Compline service. I danced. Irene danced. Maryam danced. Agnes beat the large drum steadily and slowly, and the drum's deep and guttural vibrations dominated the dark round chapel like an invisible being. I took the tom-tom and chirped a sharp quick patter. We celebrated each other while others mourned Jesus' crucifixion.

In the early 1970s, my parents would pile me and my siblings into the station wagon on Sunday morning for Mass at Saint Joseph's Catholic Church in Hopkins, a middle-class Minneapolis suburb. But sometimes we'd vary that weekly routine and head into downtown Minneapolis to the Saint Joan of Arc Church. The Catholic Diocese wanted to excommunicate Saint Joan's priest for letting women stand on the altar and read the gospel and serve communion. During one Mass, a troupe of ballet dancers performed in front of the altar. This parish had poor people, black people too, standing in the pews on Sunday. Not at Saint Joseph's, our suburban Hopkins church where my father read the First Reading almost every Sunday at the 10 o'clock Mass.

I had never questioned why we sometimes went to Mass at Saint Joan's instead of Saint Joseph's. Who propelled it? My mother? Her brother, my Uncle the Priest, had a nun friend

who had a job at Saint Joan's. After Mass, we'd wait while my mother went to find her. We all liked her. She smiled with big white teeth and wore regular clothes, not a nun's habit. Maybe I had the wrong idea about my mother. Actually, I had no idea about her thoughts on the Church. We attended Church every Sunday. Confession every Saturday too. While I was in high school, my parents taught a catechism class on Wednesday nights in the family room, next to the fireplace. I battled my mother every Wednesday before the other students arrived. I preferred to watch "One Flew Over the Cuckoo's Nest" on TV that night, not sit in my living room talking about God with teenagers. Matthew, the pimply basketball star, and Eddie, the handsome hockey goalie, were both stars at my high school, part of the popular group. Eventually, I would surrender. I sat quiet and angry on the sofa with the boys and listened to my parents discuss Catholic theology.

Perhaps my mother was an undercover religious radical or maybe the trip to Saint Joan's was my mother's ploy to get out of the suburbs and into the big city. After Mass at Saint Joan's, we'd eat lunch at Mama Rosa's Italian restaurant in Dinkytown, the University of Minnesota's hippy neighborhood. We'd sit under Mama Rosa's latticed ceiling hung with fake plastic grape vines and eat spaghetti and meatballs at a table with a wine bottle encased in rattan and covered in dripped wax from the candle stuck in its neck. After Mass at Saint Joseph's in Hopkins, we drove to the Lincoln Del in Saint Louis Park and ordered (and had to share four ways – my mother wouldn't eat) a corned beef sandwich or matzo ball soup with a side of beets, the food of my Eastern European grandparents. That cuisine made sense after sitting through an hour of Mass delivered in a heavy Czech accent by Father Benes, the parish priest.

Dancing around the simple wooden altar with my au pair friends, beating on drums, singing, watching our African friend toss her long cornrows while she performed modern dance moves, I laughed about my motley Catholic upbringing and thanked my mother for her surreptitious actions to educate us about the different types of Catholic in white-bread Minnesota of the 1970s.

Tonight's dancing was another way of being Catholic. There were no rules. And there was more than one way to find spiritual ground: both dancing with my sisters around the altar and singing Psalms at Compline every night around the altar with my other sisters, the nuns. Instead of mourning on this Good Friday, we celebrated. What would the Jesuit say about that?

CHAPTER 21

EASTER

Fifteen nuns in ivory white habits, five priests in white robes and several dozen convent guests and residents from the town of Saint Mathieu de Tréviers, stood around a bonfire burning on the gravel driveway outside the convent's central building. The sun had almost disappeared behind Saint Loup Peak. Children struggled to get out of their parent's confining arms. Adults shifted their weight back and forth and churned the white gravel under their feet. Two priests read by light from torches held by two other men in white robes. Small and sturdy Sister Dominique held a large cross, the liturgical wise woman of this community.

After this Saturday night ceremony, the nuns invited everyone to an Easter Vigil party in the lounge where we au pairs had sung together many nights after dinner over the past month. Tonight, almost midnight, we drank rich, steaming hot chocolate with small flakey croissants and Swedish cardamom rolls, moist and buttery. The meal was simple but delicious.

The next morning, I sang at the Easter Sunday Mass with Agnes, Irene and Jean-Pierre, the Chef. At Easter Sunday lunch, 50 of us, nuns and au pairs and people from town, sat in the dining room together. The bright Mediterranean sun streamed through the large picture window. The animated tables made the room feel alive, so different than the usual flat lunch meal. Christ is Risen! Hallelujah!

We started with a simple green butter lettuce salad dressed lightly with Dijon vinaigrette. A huge Norwegian salmon arrived triumphantly on a platter garnished with saffron-tinted mayonnaise. Lemon slices and dough baked into shapes to resemble the head, fins and tail of the fish had been placed anatomically-correct on and around the big fish. The local Picpoul de Pineau white wine's crisp fruit washed away the salmon's cold oiliness. The third course, ravioli, was served with a dry red Pic Saint Loup Reserve, 1998. Dessert was a simple cake with strawberries and cream.

I sat at a long table across from Sister Patrice and another bent old woman who must have lived in town and attended Mass at the convent regularly since the two women seemed like good friends. We verbally dissected the salmon and the quality of the lovely wines.

In the letter that Sister Jeanne faxed to me in Santa Barbara to accept my request to spend a month at the convent, she had described the food as "bon". I was so excited that I read the letter quickly, without much analysis. I took it to a friend at work who was French to make sure I understood exactly what the letter said I was getting myself into. My friend didn't alert me to the word "bon", another one of those French words whose interpretation depends on what it's modifying. In the food case, "bon" meant adequate or OK. It didn't mean good, as in "the food is good at the convent". The food at the convent was in fact mediocre and constipating. But on Easter Sunday, the food was not bon, it was excellent. Chris had indeed risen!

Sister Patrice turned to another old woman across from me with very bad teeth and said something about America. When I asked them what they were talking about, Sister Patrice responded "money money money." Frustrated, I turned to Agnes who looked elegant in the black sheath that didn't fit me. Did she understand everything the French said to her? She admitted she didn't and I felt relieved that I wasn't alone in my struggle with the language. I decided to let it go. If their conversation was about rich Americans, it wasn't about me anyway.

I recalled a catastrophic dinner party I attended soon after I arrived in Paris. A coworker in Santa Barbara had a sister who had lived in Paris for many years. She worked as a circus clown and lived with her boyfriend, a French academic. They asked me to join them for dinner at the apartment of the Department Head of the university where he taught.

The Circus Clown introduced me to the attractive small-boned hostess who nodded at me and then turned to air-kiss her friends. She looked about 50 and wore an Hermès blue print silk scarf around her neck. She talked with much animation and got lots of attention from her guests who nodded in obeisance. She was a sociologist, the Circus Clown told me, and a Mandarin: a high-level bureaucrat who worked for the minister of something about social affairs. Either she had two jobs or I had misunderstood or missed a crucial piece of information about the hostess. I didn't want to quiz The Mandarin about her job. I'd heard that Americans talked about their jobs at dinner parties; the French did not. I tried to relax and hoped someone would give me a drink soon.

At the dinner table, the conversation centered on academic subjects. Emboldened by two glasses of excellent red wine, I described the master's thesis I'd written almost 20 years ago, a comparative study of the French vs. American gender wage gap. I listed the historical sources I'd used to develop my hypothesis and the economists whose theories were important in my academic subject area when I wrote the theoretical tome in the mid-1980s.

"Oh, Americans – what do they know about feminism?" the hostess interrupted. I was shocked by her dismissal. Americans had a rather prominent role in the global feminist movement, I thought.

I tried to defend the American branch of feminist studies, its history and feminists but I wasn't confident with my level of the French language to express myself well, or to defend American Feminist Theory - I had written that thesis so long ago. She looked at me blankly and then turned to talk to the Polish man next to her, a visiting professor.

Apparently no one could compete with Madame Simone de Beauvoir. I felt squashed and embarrassed by Madame Le Mandarin, kicked aside with all the American feminist academics. How could the Circus Clown stand these snobby people?

When I arrived back at my apartment after midnight, I called my parents in Minneapolis. My dad answered. I cried into the phone, drunk on several glasses of red wine and cognac I had consumed to numb the insults thrown at me like daggers.

"Don't take it so seriously," he said. This was what he'd repeated since my birth as a sensitive girl.

I had always defended the French when Americans called them snobs. "How do you know? Do you know any French people? They aren't snobs – they have a major history of literature that goes back centuries. They deserve their attitude," I would say.

I couldn't believe I'd had that same experience. Madame Le Mandarin's behavior was so stereotypically French that I couldn't believe I let myself fall for it. I was crushed. I felt stupid.

But today, at Easter Lunch with the nuns, the au pairs, and the dozens from this rural community, I was not a stupid American or a second-rate feminist. And the wine was just as yummy at this Easter table as it was at that Parisian dinner party of snotty academics.

The Easter celebration at the convent continued into Sunday night.

Sister Jeanne called the Easter midnight celebration feast "Self-Service". Someone – not us au pairs - had arranged platters of ham, dried sausage slices and duck pâté on tables in the lounge. I fixated on a salad of tomatoes with fresh mozzarella cut into cubes, and sprinkled with dried basil in a balsamic vinaigrette. The buffet was colorful and abundant: the silver platters, the salads in glass bowls – and I didn't have to serve it or clean it up later. The cheese plate was loaded with enormous pieces of stinky Camembert, blue-veined Roquefort, white Chèvre, smooth Savoie, and a soft and flaky asiago-type cheese. Two different Charlottes competed as dessert. The first filled a large glass bowl with chocolate mousse that gave easily to the spoon I sank into its frothy ganache. The second Charlotte had apple slices wedged between layers of pale yellow ladyfingers and whipped cream, all mushy-sweet from contact. And local red and white wines again.

Over the weekend, two former au pairs showed up for the Easter celebration. Elsa was young, Swedish and blonde, dressed like a deb from the 1950s in a pink pencil skirt and pale yellow sweater set. Ana was Spanish, a little older, Agnes's age. Both young women seemed like good Catholic girls but Ana had a sex appeal she carried on her curvy figure and displayed in her southern Spanish accent.

I wore the only dress I had packed for France, a long navy silk patterned with small grey flower buds, and a length of pearls my ex-fiancé's parents gave me. Ana and I sat cross-legged on the floor in the crowded lounge, balancing plates of meat and cheese in our laps while we drank the local spicy white Picpoul de Pineau. Finally I had found someone who liked to drink! She had done two months at Les Tourelles five years ago and told me she had returned for Easter every year since then. I hadn't thought about coming back. She told me she didn't like her current job teaching German to engineers in Spain who worked for Mercedes Benz. She knew American folk songs, hoped she had an American accent when she spoke English, as opposed to an English one, and wanted to talk about the culture of America. With me.

The connection with Ana, all these connections I made in the convent, shifted my cells momentarily, and pulled me into the river of humanity. I didn't resist so much. I didn't want to declare that this was better than time spent alone but I noticed that I didn't need to be alone so much anymore. I remembered feeling the competition between spending my time with others and preserving time for myself when I first arrived at the convent. I still wanted to be alone but I wasn't lonely. I felt filled up.

Tonight felt like the Easters my family spent at the large Tudor-style house my favorite cousins lived in on Lake Superior in northern Minnesota. We cousins stayed up late and played Crazy Eights and Old Maid card games. I argued with my parents to let me stay up just a little longer. I didn't have to leave this party early tonight and I didn't want it to end.

My Uncle the Priest gave a sermon when I was a teenager, the only sermon of thousands he gave that I remembered, where he described Holy Communion as a meal with people, a reason to gather. The purpose of the sacrament of Communion was to gather together over food; food was the connector. Holy Communion wasn't just about eating the body and blood of Christ and getting some spiritual kick from it, it was communion with others, but he didn't state it exactly that way.

Maybe food could create world peace. Eating together, not fighting together. The Israelis and Palestinians needed to have some picnics on the Golan Heights. And men needed to eat with women.

Who did prepare that last supper for Jesus and his disciples? Now it got political. Who cooks, who gets to eat, who serves and who has to clean up. Not so easy.

At this midnight Easter celebration feast, Sister Jeanne and the other nuns wore their habits. They floated around the partyers in their long white robes and smiled like fairy hostesses. Were they happy because they had just celebrated the Resurrection of Jesus or because this was a good party? Sister Jeanne looked like a girl. Her face beamed from inside the stiff fabric that framed her face and covered her hair.

When I was at the buffet getting more wine and cheese, she told me that she'd pray for me to meet a French man, marry him and live in Paris. Then I could visit the convent on weekends! she suggested. I laughed. Maybe I would be returning someday, like Ana did. This community was now one of my families.

CHAPTER 22

EASTER MONDAY

During Easter weekend, a couple arrived in a big new light gray Lancia, the most expensive car I'd ever seen parked at the convent. They had driven from the Alsace in Northeastern France and he was in computers. Both of them were myopic - he more than she - and wore thick glasses with dark rims. His jaw line and teeth were off kilter. Her moon-shaped face sat large on her large body. They both had dark hair and looked like siblings except that he was slight and she had substantial bones.

They sat next to each other at the dining table for each meal that Easter weekend like shy people. I saw them sitting together in the chapel during evening Compline and walking the grounds of the convent hand in hand, brown heads looking at the ground, she one head taller than he.

He started to come out of his shyness at dinner in the dining room one evening but I couldn't understand what he said to me. His Alsatian accent crippled the words and his misshapen mouth prevented me from gleaning any assistance by reading his lips.

I approached the couple at the "Self-Service" post-Easter party. We didn't have a table separating us now. They stared at me through thick lenses while I described why I was here, that I was an American, spewing my advanced French with confidence. I felt like the Statue of Liberty, decked out in pearls and silk, torch glowing. They watched me while I told them about Santa Barbara's beauty, nestled between the mountains and Pacific Ocean, and my work as a land-use planner there.

I said goodbye to the couple from Alsace on the bright sunny Monday after Easter. She approached me first. I stood near the door of the doughnut-shaped building that housed the au pairs because I was in pajamas and my green silk Chinese robe. She thanked me with a quiet handshake and turned to walk across the crunchy limestone gravel to their big car. He then came forward. He kissed both my cheeks in a gentle goodbye. He had cologne on and now it was on my face. I didn't know what to say other than au revoir.

I felt like a hummingbird, lighting upon situations and people, sharing the richness of our spirits, then leaving to find another situation I could bless. None of these exchanges lasted – I was in and out before it got messy or boring. Yet these exchanges were profound. His cologne on my cheek stayed with me all day and I wondered about a man's fragility.

He had brown eyes like François's. I wasn't very nice to François. Sure, he was a little creepy but he was fragile too. I summed him up and pushed him away.

How about Eric? Was he fragile?

After Eric left me, I started going to the batting cages on advice from my homeopath. She said I needed to get the anger out of my body. I feared that someone I knew would see me so I timed my arrival at Batty's near Santa Barbara's East Beach 30 minutes before it closed at 9:00 P.M. I went so often that I should have had my own personal bat at the cages, like some did. The bat boy knew my bat size and weight. He always rented me the same one.

Exhilaration flooded my body as I hit the ball with a clean steel ping and watched it fly beautifully over the ball-spewing apparatus in the center of the circularly arrayed cages, and then disappear up into the darkness. I imagined smashing Eric's round dark head open.

But Batty's was no cure for my heartbreak; I had to keep returning. My hand bones hurt from the impact of the ball on the steel bat even though I wore my battered sailing gloves to soften the blows. Batty's was just like I remembered confession as a girl. My soul felt clean and gleaming white when I exited the confessional with a penance of three Hail Marys the priest assigned me. But the high never lasted.

Outside of sex, Eric and I spent weekends discussing the health benefits of baking salmon on a cedar plank and how he could control his cholesterol and weight. There was nothing wrong with this domestic scene but it wasn't enough for me. I wanted more than a piece of salmon and an evening spent eating it in front of a movie rented from Captain Video.

But Eric was a relief after the craziness of Troy, my previous boyfriend. After a month of dating Troy, I got a call from the Ventura police department. The officer asked me if I knew why Troy, the suspect, was at Kinko's, at midnight, wearing a false beard. I don't know, I responded. Like that night and many subsequent nights, Troy sat me down, leaned forward, and with his beautiful brown eyes, blonde-boy face and triathlete body, he convinced me to stay, despite the counterfeiting, a sexual harassment lawsuit, and inability to repay the hundreds of dollars I lent him. After he was evicted from his office, where he slept on the floor after he was evicted from his apartment, I let him move in with me. I couldn't let him go: I wanted to reform this bad boy. I believed there was something redeemable inside. But I was done when he told me that he lusted after a local radio DJ but that he couldn't ask her out; she was out of his league. So that meant I was in his league, a cheap moll to a petty criminal.

After Troy, Eric seemed normal, almost boring, fixated with his gadgets. But when I asked Eric about his spiritual beliefs, he thought my inquiry was too personal and strange. And now I was at a convent.

A Santa Barbara friend didn't understand either. "Why do you want to stay in a convent?" she asked a second time. What I didn't tell her was that I fled to the convent. I was stir-crazy for out, for something new, for anonymity, for a jolt. I fled the work schedule, friends, shopping for groceries, and keeping busy. My life was tedious and full of too much, a summation of emptiness. The convent seemed logical too: it preserved my small budget and fed my love of frugality.

The week before I left Santa Barbara, a friend declared that I had a beautiful life: art, music and physical beauty surrounded me. She observed the scene from my little yellow kitchen and calculated my apartment. Seven women filled my studio, all speaking French. They tentatively hovered over the sofa and chairs I had for them to sit on. When I looked again, they had taken hold of the chairs and sofa and leaned toward each other, speaking energetically.

I did have a beautiful life but I wanted more. I sought the convent to be born again, but not religiously. California offered spiritual respite in its vast open spaces, in sunsets or oceans or mountains but its fix was always temporary. I wanted to absorb the cathedrals and monasteries, to stand on land where religious history happened, to stew in it for a while.

Reprendre Souffle. I reread the brochure as I sat on my little bed. My suitcases were filled with Princesse Tam Tams, my heavy Doc Martens, the Patagonia fleece sweatshirt that Eric gave me, my laptop, journals, photos, Chinese robe, and tea. I had to take it all back home with me.

I would take this couple with me too. They had a spiritual connection I'd never experienced with a man. Sex connected me to my lover but I wanted more than that. I wanted what they had, brown heads bowed in the bright sun, walking slowly around the convent together, partners.

Agnes had lent me her Walkman on my last night at the convent and I listened to her Moravian music CD while I packed. A frog stuck to the outside of my window, bright green in the black night. It hung on for several hours, keeping me company.

After dinner that evening, Agnes and I dried and stacked warm thin white dishes fresh out of the robot dishwasher. "I'm in love with an African priest," Agnes confessed. She had met him in Brighton during a Catholic event for young people. He was ready to leave his priestly studies for her.

"Where would we live?" she frowned, holding a threadbare drying cloth and wet glass in her hands. "A black man and white woman can't live in the Czech Republic. Africa is too far away from my family in Litomyšl." She looked at the linoleum floor. I was stunned. "Paris?" I suggested. "New York?"

As I started packing, Irene knocked on my cell door. She told me she wanted to say good-bye without the rest of the team around. She sat on my bed with me and told me about her sad love life at 19: affairs with a 30-year old volleyball trainer and a 25-year old journalist. Both had told her to keep the relationships secret. She worried that others thought she was a slut.

The next morning, I took a picture of the grapevines outside of my window for the last time. It was cold and rainy and the grape leaves bursted with color and vigor. The clean cool air woke me up and cleared a veil of the cloudiness from my head. I was ready for my next adventure.

CHAPTER 23

EYRES-MONCUBE

The next morning, Sister Jeanne miraculously consented to let Irene use the convent's Peugeot to take me into Montpellier to pick up a rental car. I planned to drive southwest, into the Pyrenees Mountains, into the land of foie gras and stone monasteries of the tenth and eleventh centuries.

As we drove down the hill away from the convent, after a month of Lent, I had to be honest with myself: I hadn't accomplished my grand plan. True, I had followed my dream by coming to France, but I had also had high hopes of spending the month in the convent writing down what I had done with my life, with men, my jobs, to find patterns and clues of what I should do next. But still, it wasn't a mistake that I happened to come to the convent during the dark liturgical season of Lent and left right after the Resurrection.

I drove west into Aquitaine, the historic land of Eleanor. At 10:00 P.M., I called a convent from a pay phone sitting at a junction of two one-lane roads on the outskirts of Mont-de-Marsan, a town with no French charm, so unattractive that the Michelin Guide didn't even list any sights worth seeing here. It was getting dark and I was panicked. I had just hung up the phone after calling another convent whose response to my request for a room was that they didn't house overnight guests. No room at that inn.

This nun asked no questions. In response to my request to spend the night, she told me how to find the convent, outside the village of Eyres-Moncube. "At the roundabout, go toward Saint Sever, then left to Pau," she explained. I drove into the darkness, trying to remember the directions the nun had given me. I prayed that I'd be guided.

There was nothing to sense in the pitch black except the smell of animal manure and the sound of my pounding heart. My headlights illuminated the white wooden signs stacked at intersections to indicate direction just as I drove past them. I backed up in the dark to read the names of tiny towns printed in black. Then there were no indicators. No more signs to guide me.

When I saw a light up ahead on the right, the only light other than my headlights on the narrow roadway's blacktop, I knew I had found the convent. The light shone over a door and illuminated a little cross above it – a sure sign of nun habitation. No lights on inside.

It was so dark that I couldn't make out what kind of convent structure I parked in front of. I rang the bell and cringed at the sound it made in the absolute silence. The door opened to a tall, large-faced nun, covered in white, her pale face framed by the hexagon formed by the habit's stiff headpiece. She instructed me to drive my car back out to the road. I looked out to nothing but a black curtain. "Turn into the next drive; I'll meet you there," she instructed.

Inside the converted barn, she explained that others were sleeping here too: a handyman and the mother of one of the nuns in this community of Dominicans. More Dominicans, but these were truly cloistered Dominicans, unlike my nuns at the convent in Languedoc. I would not see any of these nuns other than this large one.

After she showed me my room, the nun insisted on feeding me, even though it was late, almost midnight. I stood awkwardly at a long table in the middle of an open room while I waited for her to return. The oddly-pitched ceiling made the room feel unbalanced. Faded travel posters covered the walls. I wondered which anonymous doors contained the handyman and the nun's mother. I was nervous that my flushing the toilet would wake them.

I watched her set down a tray with a plate of soggy green beans and a piece of gray meat, along with a few pieces of stale bread in a basket. A Catholic newsmagazine sat next to my place setting, its pages turned to an article describing a candidate for sainthood who was recently discovered in Poland. I listened to her excitedly tell me this breaking news. Was this a test? Was I really a Catholic? Could she tell that I was an imposter? I nodded my head, sat down and thanked her. Then she left me alone.

I woke up early the next morning in a double bed that sagged in the middle. The uneven cement floor, painted a worn-away rust color, felt cool under my bare feet. A small

yellow rag rug lay tired next to the bed. The room was large but so bare and modest compared to my cell at the Tourelles convent with its red stone tiled floor and modern sink and shower.

My room's large window opened to blonde wheat fields and a sagging clothesline. The sloping grade of newly plowed fields of black dirt recalled the terrain of my grandmother's farm in southeastern Minnesota. It smelled like her farm too: fresh manure and the yeasty-sour smell of recently cut hay.

I was aware of the angle of the sun. I realized that I was at about the same latitude from the equator as her farm was: 43 degrees. Her farm sat less than a mile from the Iowa State Line and I was now nowhere near Iowa, but I wasn't surprised that I had ended up here at this poor rural convent. Like the dream had felt, this terrain felt familiar too, truly an echo from the past.

I stayed a second night. I ate the very simple dinner of potatoes and gravy-soaked meat with my barn-mates. This meal made the Tourelles convent food taste Michelin-starred, even the fare we were served during Lent.

After dinner, before the sun set completely, I walked down the middle of a newly asphalted road, corn on one side, dense forest on the other. Signs nailed to the trees stated that the land was banned to hunters. I wondered if these land preserves were trespassable by a hiker. Would a French farmer shoot me if he saw me walking in his forest? I stayed on the asphalt.

Under the dark pink streak of clouds, I could hear a tractor plowing the black dirt. The sound of the motor took me back to southern Minnesota again, to my grandmother's farm, a region that looked exactly like Eyres-Moncube: rolling land, black dirt, and large patches of forest that the tractors left standing. And the steady wind - it took me back so fast and so completely that I felt my grandmother was with me.

During those childhood summers on my grandmother's farm, I made certain decisions about life. I developed fantasies of love and romance as I roamed the apple orchards and threaded my way through tall corn stalks. Those fantasies hadn't changed much since then. Perhaps my desire to visit the cheesemonger's farm in Normandy wasn't about being lonely, but wanting to reconnect with my younger and less jaded self.

While I was a student at Saint Teresa's College, my grandmother would sometimes drive the 50 miles from the farm to rescue me from another disappointing weekend in Winona. Instead of meeting preppy boys like handsome David at the few parties I attended at Saint Mary's, I drank beer with a stoned philosophy student who wore dirty jeans with ragged hems that dragged on the ground. He said goodbye in the lobby of my dormitory by running his hands up and down my body. I could smell the weed on his face as he lunged in for a clumsy kiss while a nun waited to check me in for the night.

Back at the poor convent, my barn-mates asked me where I was planning to travel when I left tomorrow morning. I walked out to my car to find a map to show them my route west to the region of Landes. The handyman followed me.

In the absolute pitch dark, with only the stars as illumination, the handyman and I leaned on a wooden fence next to each other and looked out to the dark fields. He told me that he had few options to make a living. He was 50, single and the unemployment rate was high in rural France. So he took care of the convent. He was thin and tall, with a stiff shock of gray hair. I was surprised he divulged his personal life to me, an American woman, a stranger.

While he spoke, I watched the stars get brighter and brighter.

Out of habit, I located the Big Dipper, easy to do since I'd done it most of my life. As a girl, I followed my father outside into the night to a place in the road in front of our house that let us see the sky, clear of trees. He pointed to the constellation's rhombus and I followed its bowl up and over its lip to an imagined line that led straight to the North Star.

I had followed my dream to France, and to a convent. Though I appeared as a nun in my dream, I had never intended to become one. And the dream didn't predict that I'd find a community of women that fed me, more than any man could, or had yet. The dream had me take a different route, one to France, to a place where I took the time to breathe. Reprendre Souffle: a different kind of praying. In my desperation to end my loneliness and single state, I found myself, with an interior that was strong, like the dream nun.

While this man next to me shared his story, I wasn't considering what he could give me as a potential partner, if he could fill me up, if he could rescue me. Like the nun in the dream, that desperation was now absent.

I would leave him here. Like the dream nun, I no longer had to figure out how to get him. Even if he had been rich, I wanted to continue my journey alone, at least for a little while. I wasn't a nun!

I had the convent inside of me now, so unlike the dream convent with its medieval courtyard and cathedral. When I needed to, I could return to my inner convent, for a refresher course.

At 43 degrees latitude, in the middle of nowhere France, I looked into an infinite North. My body hummed with calm strength, rooting me to something ancient and holy. It was the same feeling I had experienced while sitting under sunlit stained glass in Parisian churches and when singing Psalm 93 in the convent chapel with the nuns. I looked up at the millions of stars and stood surrounded by their illumination, like under the ceiling of a cathedral.

THE END

Acknowledgements

Thank you to Patricia Hampl, Mary Carroll Moore, Deborah Bushinski, and my Santa Barbara Writing Group who got me started, and my San Francisco writing communities who kept me going including Maryann Miller, Caroline Wampole, The Grotto, and Litquake. Finally, I thank Cynthia Clark and her Terry Circle Writer's Refuge, the Novato Marin County Free Library and Meryl Kaleida, who helped me realize it.

About the Author

Elizabeth Podolinsky's essays on travel, food and health have been published in *The Santa Barbara Independent Weekly*, and *Healing Retreats and Spas Magazine*. She was featured at Litquake, the San Francisco literary festival. An economist for the State of California, Elizabeth has also worked as a wedding DJ, film traffic director, and tax expert for the Minnesota Legislature. She lives in San Francisco.

www.ingramcontent.com/pod-product-compliance
Lightning Source LLC
Chambersburg PA
CBHW071729080526
44588CB00013B/1960